THE
ESSENTIAL
DARKROOM
BOOK

THE ESSENTIAL DARKROOM BOOK

Tom Grill and Mark Scanlon

FOUNTAIN PRESS

Fountain Press Ltd.
65 Victoria Street,
Windsor,
Berkshire SL4 1EH,
England.

First published in the UK by Fountain Press Ltd, 1983
ISBN 0 86343 000 7.

Copyright © 1981 by Radial Press, Inc.
Photographs copyright © 1981 by Tom Grill.

First published in New York, New York, by American Photographic
Book Publishing: an imprint of Watson-Guptill Publications, a
division of Billboard Publications, Inc., 1515 Broadway, New
York, N.Y. 10036.

Designed by Tom Grill.

Printed and bound in Spain by
Graficromo S.A. Cordoba.

CONTENTS

THE ESSENTIAL DARKROOM BOOK

A Complete Guide to Black & White and Colour Processing

INTRODUCTION

Of all the creative excitement inherent in photography, few thrills surpass that of watching prints form in a darkroom dish. Even the most experienced darkroom maestro can still recall the excitement he or she felt standing for the first time under the surrealistic glow of a darkroom safe-light and marvelling at the miraculous appearance of an image.

As a photographer who does his or her own processing, you are a participant in a long "do-it-yourself" tradition that harks back to a time when photographers had no choice but to process personally the photographs they took. The luxury of taking a photograph and processing it at leisure simply did not exist then. When the darkroom craft was in its infancy, the instability that characterized many of the light-sensitive materials often demanded that processing be performed immediately after an exposure had been made. Therefore, the field of photography was limited to those people who were as adept at chemistry as they were interested in taking pictures.

Eventually, more stable chemicals were developed, commercial labs were established, and it became possible to let a specialist handle the processing. As a result, photography began to appeal on a large scale to people who previously had been discouraged by the complexities of working with darkroom chemicals.

Considering the ready availability of inexpensive commercial processing laboratories, why then does do-it-yourself processing flourish among photographers and continue to gain new and enthusiastic practitioners? The answer is found in the tremendous personal satisfaction and pride they derive from being master of all facets of a photograph – from its conception as an image, through its capture on film, to its visual realization as a print or slide.

The *Essential Darkroom Book* is designed to help you develop the skills necessary for *you* to experience the same pleasures of do-it-yourself processing that so many others have enjoyed. However, darkroom processing involves not only skills but also decisions, some of which may have to be made even before you know enough about processing to be certain what your needs will be. For example, although fundamental principles of processing are the same both in black and white and in colour, the two require somewhat different equipment. Traditionally, photographers have first purchased black-and-white processing equipment and later switched to colour. However, if you are certain that you will eventually want to engage in colour processing, the most economical approach in the long run may be to purchase the more expensive colour equipment at the outset. You may thus avoid ultimately having to incur switch-over expenses.

Moreover, when you process colour film or make colour prints, further decisions await you. Different procedures and "chemistries" exist for developing slides, for developing negatives, and for making prints from each. When you walk into a photographic dealers, you must

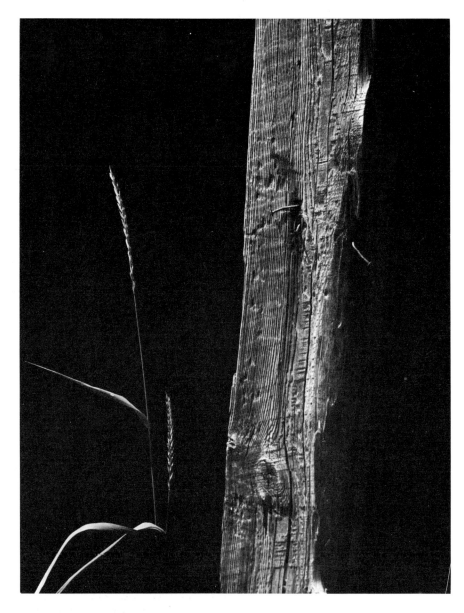

A succession of decisions contribute to the way a photograph finally appears. The succession begins when an image is framed in the viewfinder of a camera, proceeds through the development process, and culminates when the image is manipulated and projected onto a sheet of printing paper.

The decisions that affect photographic images being handled by commercial processing laboratories are often made by machines. These machines are calibrated to produce "average" results and consequently, except in the case of laboratories which cater to the needs of professional photographers, commercial labs cannot produce the exceptional results that are easily within the reach of the home processor.

know which procedures for which you will need supplies, as well as which specific brands you want to purchase.

Because there is more to learning darkroom processing than simply following "recipes," we have designed the *Essential Darkroom Book*, not only to teach you skills, but also to provide you with information with which you can make decisions such as those described above. If you have never before processed film or made prints, we suggest that before you purchase a single item of equipment, you read this book to obtain the background to darkroom processing. Because colour processing has recently been simplified to the point where learning to process colour materials is not much more difficult than learning to process black-and-white materials, you may decide to skip black-and-white processing altogether. But you will not know if that is the best course for you unless you have some understanding of the differences between the two types of processing. By reading over the entire book you can decide, and once you have made your decision, you can go back and re-read the information on specific chemistries and brands. Then, when you enter a store to outfit your darkroom, you will be an educated consumer who does not have to rely on a sales assistant for advice.

If you have had some darkroom experience in the past, in all likelihood that experience was with black-and-white processing, and you now would like to learn about colour. If that is the case, you may still want to review the black-and-white chapters first, since they are referred to in the colour chapters.

Because of the enormous popularity and widespread use of the 35mm camera, the *Essential Darkroom Book* concentrates almost exclusively on 35mm film. Although some specific items of equipment and the quantity of chemicals involved differ when processing film in sizes other than 35mm, the same basic procedures apply to developing film and making prints no matter what the size. You should encounter few, if any, problems in transferring 35mm techniques to other film sizes.

As well as providing fundamental information about darkroom processing and equipment, the *Essential Darkroom Book* also presents you with advance information on the most recent and sophisticated technological aids available. Although some of these aids may be initially too expensive or complex to be practical, they are included so that you will be aware of their availability as you hone your skills and expand your ambitions.

We have arranged the book so that procedures common to many processes are, for the most part, described only once. However, we have occasionally included information in more than one location for clarity's sake. We trust you will find these repetitions a convenience as well as an aid to your understanding.

Our goal is to give you the knowledge you need to process film and make prints successfully – even on your first attempt. We are confident that once you have watched your print materialize in a processing tray, you, too, will share in the feeling of satisfaction and pride that so many before you have enjoyed.

1. EQUIPMENT

The foundation of a good darkroom is the enlarger. For casual processing, relatively inexpensive condenser enlargers are readily available which can often be obtained second hand. More expensive diffusion enlargers, such as the one with the dichroic head shown at left, are particularly useful for colour printing, although image sharpness may suffer slightly.

The truly serious darkroom enthusiast for whom price is subordinate to image quality might opt for the unsurpassed quality obtainable from a large format enlarger, such as the one shown above. Although designed primarily to accommodate 4″ x 5″ (10 x 13 cm) negatives, such enlargers can be easily adapted to small format use with results that represent the ultimate in image reproduction.

Anybody can process film. Anybody can develop prints – in black and white or colour. Although darkroom processing may seem mysterious or intimidating or impossible to learn, it is not. With surprisingly little effort, and without much special equipment, you can master the techniques quickly, and, sooner than you might imagine, you will begin producing results that are not simply good – but great.

Many photographers believe that they need elaborate facilities and expensive equipment to obtain quality results. In fact, elaborate equipment which does most of the thinking for you can prevent you from learning the fundamental principles that you must master if you are ever to become more than a technician in the darkroom. And some of the world's most highly regarded photographic prints were created in improvised darkrooms, using primitive or outmoded equipment. Certainly good equipment can be an asset, but rest assured that you can do without if you must. It is *darkroom discipline, correct technique*, and *careful attention to detail*, more than a fortune spent on expensive equipment, that are the hallmarks of a successful darkroom maestro. Although you should buy the best equipment you can afford, in the long run it is the care that you take to develop precise and proper habits that will be the primary criteria for your success.

Many products are commercially available to help with nearly every aspect of darkroom processing. All you really need in order to produce excellent results are a few essential items. Because the enlarger is always the centre of activity, Chapter One begins with a description of enlargers and then deals in turn with additional items of equipment that you will need in order to establish a functioning darkroom. More sophisticated equipment is also described so that when you are ready to expand your darkroom, you can do so knowledgeably.

THE ENLARGER

Condenser Enlarger

The Dichroic Lamphead

A. Light source.
B. Heat shield in condenser enlarger and dichroic filters in the colour head below.
C. Condenser in the top diagram and diffuser glass in the lower.
E. Lens.

An inexpensive enlarger on the left is fitted with a filter drawer above the condenser while the one on the right has a colour head. Below is a close-up of a more sophisticated colour head fitted with dichroic filters that are simply 'dialled' in as required. There is no condenser and the light is diffused.

The two most widely used enlarger types are the condenser-head enlarger and the dichroic-head enlarger.

In a condenser-head enlarger (top), light from a tungsten bulb, A, passes through a heat-absorbing glass, B, and is focused by condenser lenses, C, onto a negative or slide, D. The light then passes through the negative or slide through an enlarger lens, E, and onto printing paper.

In a dichroic-head enlarger (lower) light from a quartz lamp, A, passes through three dichroic filters, B, which introduce the colours yellow, magenta, and cyan. The coloured light then proceeds into a diffusion chamber, C, where the colours are mixed before being directed through a negative or slide, D. An enlarger lens, E, then projects the image onto printing paper. The amount of each colour added by the dichroic filters depends on how far each filter is made to protrude into the light path.

Condenser heads produce sharp images showing high contrast and are especially well suited for black and white printing. Dichroic heads produce "softer" images of somewhat lower contrast than condenser heads and are well suited to printing in colour.

NEGATIVE CARRIERS
Film carriers are used to hold negatives and slides firmly within an enlarger. Carriers are sold in a variety of formats to accommodate different sizes of film. Some carriers merely support the edges of the film, others support the entire frame within a sandwich of glass. The glass holds the film perfectly flat but must occasionally be cleaned.

The enlarger head
The head of an enlarger is its most important and expensive component. There are three types of heads: condenser, diffusion, and cold-light.

Condenser heads
These heads use optical elements (lenses) to focus light from the enlarger lamp through the film negative and onto the printing paper (see illustration at far left). The primary shortcoming of condenser heads is their tendency to make more obvious the effects of dust, scratches, and any imperfections present in the negative.

Diffusion heads
These heads produce a "softer" (less focused) light than condenser heads, by either passing light through a diffusion glass or reflecting light back and forth in a mixing chamber (see illustration at far left).

Two types of lamp are available as light sources in condenser and diffusion heads. Condenser heads and the diffusion head that uses a diffusion glass both commonly contain a tungsten bulb, while the mixing-chamber diffusion head usually contains a quartz-halogen bulb. Both bulbs are suitable for use with black-and-white film, but the quartz-halogen bulb retains a more consistent colour balance throughout its life and is therefore especially appropriate for colour printing.

Cold-light heads
These heads employ a "cold" light source – usually a fluorescent lamp – to provide the softest, most even illumination of all. Cold lights have the unique advantage of producing so little heat that the negative or slide is in no danger of buckling when the lamp is on. Cold-light heads are expensive and therefore impractical for ordinary use.

The bellows
By expanding and contracting the bellows on an enlarger, you move the enlarger's lens up and down and thereby focus the projected image.

The lens
In order to obtain the best image possible, choose a lens of focal length approximately equal to the diagonal of a single frame of your film. (For 35mm film, you will want a lens of about 50mm focal length).

Because of the bellows component, enlarger lenses do not contain a focusing mechanism and are therefore inexpensive when compared to camera lenses. Since the quality of the image your enlarger can produce is directly affected by the quality of its lens, purchase the best lens you can afford.

The column
In order to adjust the size of the image projected by the enlarger head, you adjust the position of the head by sliding it up and down a metal column. The longer the column, the greater the degree of magnification the enlarger can produce.

The baseboard
The enlarger baseboard serves as an anchor for the column and as the surface on which you work. To produce quality prints, the head, lens, and baseboard of your enlarger must all be in perfect alignment; otherwise, the image will be distorted and you will find it difficult, if not impossible, to focus all parts of the image at once.

Format
Each enlarger has a limit to the size of negative it can accommodate. Some enlargers can only accept negatives up to 35mm in size; others can accept negatives as large as 4″ x 5″ (10 x 13 cm), 5″ x 7″ (13 x 18 cm), and even 8″ x 10″ (20 x 25 cm). In general, the larger the film format that the enlarger can handle, the more sturdily the enlarger is constructed. For most people, an enlarger that can accommodate a format as large as 2¼″ x 2¾″ (6 x 7 cm) provides adequate versatility and strikes a reasonable compromise between sturdiness and bulk.

THE COLOUR ENLARGER

Filtration Knobs, for dialing in yellow, magenta, and cyan

Area for Light Source and Dichroic Filters

Filtration Display, for showing how much of each colour has been dialed into the filter pack

Diffusion Chamber Area

White Light Lever, used to temporarily remove the colour filters from the light path, making it easier to see and focus the image on the easel

Film Carrier

Focusing Knob

Film-Carrier Release Lever

Knobs for detaching the lens from the bellows

Lens

THE COLOUR HEAD

Most enlargers suitable for black-and-white printing can be converted for colour use; however, some convert more readily, and some produce better colour prints than others. If you are certain that you will only be printing in black and white, then any high-quality condenser head with a good lens will be sufficient for your needs. If you think you may eventually want to try colour printing, or if you want to start immediately with colour, then you should be aware of the ways in which enlargers used for black-and-white printing differ from those used for colour. You should also be familiar with the accessories you will need to have on hand when making colour prints, the most important being colour filters.

Heat-absorbing glass

In order to protect colour filters, slides, and negatives from infra-red radiation, colour enlargers must pass light originating from the lamp through a heat-absorbing glass. Many enlargers contain heat-absorbing glass as original equipment, some enlargers are manufactured to accommodate it as an option, and some make no provision for such glass at all. If you ever wish to print in colour, be certain your enlarger either contains heat-absorbing glass already or can at least accept it. (Heat-absorbing glass has no effect on black and white prints.)

Supplementary colour filters

To print in colour, you must place colour filters between the enlarger's light source and the printing paper. The way enlargers accommodate such filters varies and can affect the quality of the final print.

1. *Filters under lens.* The most rudimentary method for adding filters is to attach a special filter holder to the enlarger lens. Since filters placed in such holders are inserted *between* the slide or negative and the printing paper, you must use high-quality, expensive colour-compensating (CC) filters to minimize image distortion. Unfortunately, because CC filters are made of soft gelatin and are easily scratched, they deteriorate with use and must be replaced occasionally. The chief advantage of below-the-lens filters is that when used in conjunction with an ultra-violet filter (see below) and heat-absorbing glass, they permit you to print in colour without purchasing a special enlarger head.

2. *Filter drawer.* Enlargers specifically designed to accommodate colour filters contain a built-in filter drawer. Because such drawers are situated *above* the slide or negative, the image does not project through the filters and you can use economical colour-printing (CP) filters made of acetate, instead of the more expensive CC filters.

Both types of enlarger require that you have an ample supply of CC or CP filters on hand (see p. 104). In addition, you will need to have an ultra-violet (UV) filter to screen out UV light emanating from the enlarger lamp.

3. *Dichroic heads.* Dichroic enlarger heads (which are a type of diffusion head) are designed specifically to make colour filtration convenient and precise. Dichroic heads contain internal filters which add colour to the light source in amounts you can easily control by turning dials. Moreover, the dials are calibrated in density increments of one unit – unlike CC and CP filters, which are commonly available in increments no smaller than five units. As you might expect, dichroic heads are relatively expensive, but they are unsurpassed in precision and ease of use for colour printing.

A 36-frame roll of film is approximately 4′ (1.2 m) in length and must be rolled into a shape convenient for darkroom processing. In order to insure that developing chemicals can circulate freely around all parts of the film, you coil it onto a reel and then insert the reel in a light-tight, leak-proof developing tank. The chemical processes involved in film development then take place within the tank.

FILTERS UNDER THE LENS
Filter holders enable you to introduce filters below the lens of enlargers that do not contain a filter drawer built into the enlarger head. Some enlargers are sold with a filter holder already attached below the lens.

HEAT-ABSORBING GLASS
If you plan to use your condenser enlarger for colour printing, you must be certain your enlarger contains a sheet of heat-absorbing glass to protect your negative or slide from heat damage. Most modern condenser enlargers are sold with the glass already installed, or they at least contain a slot to accept one. If your enlarger lacks a heat-absorbing glass you can probably order one from the manufacturer. The glass may be left in at all times since it has no detrimental effect on black-and-white printing.

FILTER DRAWER
Most modern condenser enlargers have a drawer built into the enlarger head in which you can place colour filters. The combination of filters placed in the drawer is referred to as the *filter* pack.

17

REELS AND TANKS

METAL REELS AND TANKS
For durability and ease of cleaning, metal developing tanks and reels are unsurpassed.

Tanks are sold in various capacities, ranging from single-reel tanks to tanks that can handle ten or more reels at once. Since you must fill a tank completely with chemicals regardless of how many rolls of film you are processing, you may want to keep a few different tank sizes on hand.

Some photographers who do a substantial amount of processing store their chemicals inside extra tanks and then place loaded film reels directly into the chemicals. This method saves time and, in the case of multi-reel tanks, allows all the reels to begin development almost simultaneously.

Two different sizes of metal reels are shown above. Be sure the tanks and reels you purchase fit the film size you are using.

REELS

Metals reels

Stainless steel reels are designed for durability and ease of cleaning. Mounting film on metal reels can be a somewhat tricky procedure at first, but once you have mastered the technique, metal reels are the most convenient type available. Although metal reels are comparatively expensive, they last so long and are so easy to clean and dry that they are worth the extra cost.

Plastic reels

To make loading film onto reels easier and to offer a less expensive alternative to metal reels, some manufacturers produce reels constructed of plastic. Initially, plastic reels may seem easier to load, but the many grooves characteristic of the reels make cleaning and drying them a slow process. With practice, you will be able to load both metal and plastic reels with equal ease, so buy plastic reels only if you truly cannot afford metal ones.

TANKS

Metal tanks

As is the case with reels, stainless steel tanks are both more durable and more expensive than their plastic counterparts. Since the temperature of the chemicals in a tank must sometimes be adjusted by immersing the tank in a water bath, metal tanks have the advantage of transmitting temperature changes quickly.

Plastic tanks

Plastic tanks cost only one-quarter to one-third the price of metal tanks, but they are far more likely to crack or break. Moreover, most plastic tanks can hold only one reel of film at a time, whereas metal tanks allow you to process as many as ten reels at once.

Hybrid tanks

Sometimes metal tanks with metal tops leak slightly around the rim. Because plastic can establish a better seal than metal, hybrid tanks consisting of a metal tank with a plastic top combine the best features of both.

PLASTIC REELS AND TANKS
This inexpensive tank, reel, and thermometer kit is almost a complete film-processing darkroom in itself. The reel adjusts to handle more than one film size and possesses a rachet device to make film loading simple. However, tanks of this type can handle only one roll at a time, and for reasons discussed in the text, plastic tanks and reels are better suited for developing an occasional roll of film than for serious and frequent use.

If you want to try your hand at film developing to see if you enjoy it, but want to keep your initial investment to a minimum, plastic processing tanks and reels may be worthwhile.

SAFELIGHTS

SAFELIGHTS

Visible light consists of a broad range of colours. Because some films and printing papers are not affected by certain of those colours, you need not operate in total darkness. You can use a "safelight" to provide dim illumination that will not ruin the light-sensitive material with which you are working.

Safelight colours

The correct safelight colour to use varies from film to film and paper to paper. For most black-and-white papers, a light amber bulb (coded OC by Kodak and 902 by Ilford) is standard. Always check the instructions provided by a material's manufacturer before you assume that it can be viewed under a particular safelight (or any safelight at all, for that matter).

Intensity

Even a safelight of the correct colour can affect a film or paper if it is located too close or is too strong. As a rule, the light source should never be closer than 4' (1.2 m) from any light-sensitive material, and the bulb should be no stronger than 15 watts.

Duration of exposure

Some papers and most films can only be exposed to a safelight for a limited time without a chemical change taking place. Check the manufacturer's instructions, and follow them carefully. Although some manufacturers claim that their colour printing paper can be viewed under an amber light or that their panchromatic black-and-white film can be viewed under a dark green light, not all films and papers have these qualities. In any event, the illuminations recommended in the instances above are so dim that they are of little help.

Selection

Safelights are sold in a variety of designs, sizes, and prices. Base your selection on the size and configuration of your darkroom, and on the type of illumination – spot or general – that you want. Dome lights are best for spot lighting; flat, round, and two-sided lights are best for large areas. Recently, coated bulbs that simply screw into a conventional light socket have been improved to the point where they are now a reasonable and economical source of general safelight illumination. If you think you will need

A simple but effective darkroom lamp which employs a coloured translucent cover over a low wattage bulb. It is suitable for most purposes except colour processing.

THE DOME SAFELIGHT
Dome safelights such as the one shown above allow you to direct light onto a specific area, such as a developer tray or the area where you store your paper. By concentrating light, dome safelights help prevent stray light from interfering with your ability to see and focus the image projected by your enlarger. An added advantage is that many dome lights accept filters, so they can be adapted for use with more than one type of paper.

more than one safelight colour, safelights with changeable filters are available.

These sections of your darkroom that do not involve the use of chemicals constitute its "dry side". In addition to your enlarger, the items you should consider buying in order to outfit your darkroom's dry side properly are discussed below.

SAFELIGHT FILTERS

Safelight Filter Colour	Kodak Code	Use For
Light amber	OC	Most b/w printing papers
Amber	No. 13	Ektacolor 74 RC paper
Dark amber	No. 10	Panalure
Green	No. 3	b/w panchromatic films

DRYSIDE EQUIPMENT
Masking Frames

1. *Four-blade, fully adjustable masking frame.* Fully adjustable masking frames permit you to crop a photograph from all four sides, thereby allowing you to centre the image on your paper regardless of how wide you make the borders.

2. *Borderless masking frame.* Borderless easels hold printing paper firmly but do not form a border on the print. The sliding paper guides on the left and right adjust to accommodate different paper sizes. The easel shown here has been painted black to make it non-reflective.

3. *Simple easel.* The simplest type of masking frame accepts only one size of paper and produces only one border size. These masking frames are useful for masking many identical prints from the same negative or slide.

4. *Two-blade adjustable easel.* Two-blade adjustable masking frames permit unlimited cropping along two edges, but the other two edges can only be varied from about $\frac{1}{8}''$ (.3 cm) to about $\frac{3}{8}''$ (.9 cm).

5. *Large adjustable borderless masking frame.* The borderless masking frame holds the printing paper on only two edges. Oversize prints need to be held on all four edges to keep the paper flat. Paper slipped into the upper left corner of the large adjustable borderless masking frame is held along two edges by fixed rails and along the remaining two edges by movable rails.

Masking Frame

If you lay a piece of paper on your enlarger's baseboard while making an exposure, the paper's natural tendency to curl will ruin the image you are attempting to reproduce. By holding the paper flat, a masking frame assures you that the image will be undistorted, in sharp focus, and will not move during the exposure. A variety of masking frames are available.

Fixed-size masking frames

Fixed-size masking frames accept paper of a single size (4″ x 5″, 5″ x 7″, etc.) and are most useful for printing many copies of the one size quickly. They are inexpensive and automaitcally produce a narrow white border around the print.

Borderless masking frames

Borderless masking frames enable you to print on an entire sheet of paper without wasting any space on a border. These masking frames are moderate in cost.

Adjustable-border masking frames

Masking frames with adjustable borders are available in two types. The more expensive type is adjustable on all four sides and allows you to produce an image completely surrounded by a border of any size. The less expensive "corner-adjustable" type has only two sides that are movable. Corner-adjustable masking frames allow you to crop your photograph to any size by changing the position of two sides, but the size of the border can only be changed from about $\frac{1}{8}''$ to $\frac{1}{2}''$ (.3 to 1.3 cm).

Multiprint masking frames

Multiprint masking frames contain several openings of varying sizes which enable you to print more than one image on a single sheet of paper.

Selecting a masking frame

When deciding on which masking frame to buy, select one that will accommodate the largest sheet of paper you expect to use. Judge a masking frame by how securely it holds a sheet of paper and how easily you can load it in the dark. A good masking frame will greatly simplify your printing labours.

Timers

TIMERS

If you are to obtain consistent results from print to print, you must have a device that will turn your enlarger on and off accurately during exposures. Enlarger timers range from the simple to the sophisticated.

Mechanical timers

Mechanical timers are the least expensive timers available and are certainly adequate for most darkrooms.

Digital timers

Digital timers employ electronic circuitry to produce extreme, and usually unneeded, accuracy. Some digital timers are designed to turn off the darkroom safelight automatically while you focus the enlarger image (making it easier to see the image on the easel); others can be set to signal when to begin "dodging" or "burning in" (see p. 76).

Programmable timers

Some timers can be set to produce a sequence of different time intervals. A programming capability is rarely useful when exposing prints but can be very handy when developing either film or prints.

Selecting a timer

When selecting a timer, your main consideration should be that it repeats the same time interval accurately. If your budget permits, look for a timer that can be preset to repeat the same interval over and over.

MECHANICAL TIMERS (above)
The simple mechanical timer shown here is inexpensive but perfectly adequate for most common darkroom needs. The timer contains some electrical circuitry which permits it to turn the enlarger on and off.

PROGRAMMABLE TIMERS (opposite)
Because darkroom processing usually involves a series of timed steps, programmable timers have been developed which can be preset to time each step sequentially.
　　The timer at left can be programmed for the whole sequence of steps in any process by inserting the pins in appropriate positions. As the dial turns and a pin reaches the twelve o'clock position, a bell rings and the timer stops. Timing does not begin for the next step until the bar along the bottom edge of the timer is depressed.

ELECTRICAL TIMERS (opposite)
The type of timer shown at left is the "workhorse" of electrical darkroom timers. The enlarger and darkroom safelight can be connected into this type of timer so that all on-off functions are controlled by the timer. The large, luminescent dial is easy to read in the dark, and depending on how the timer is set, it can produce audible ticks or ring a bell when a timing period expires.

VOLTAGE REGULATORS

Household electrical current fluctuates enough from second to second to affect the intensity of light emanating from your enlarger lamp. These fluctuations usually have little noticeable effect on black and white prints, but with colour prints, even minor variations in exposure can produce significant colour shifts. Therefore, to smooth out voltage variations, colour printing usually calls for a voltage regulator to be attached to your enlarger. Many dichroic enlarger heads are sold with a voltage regulator already installed, but you should check to be certain, in the event you find yourself obtaining inconsistent results in your colour prints.

DRYSIDE EQUIPMENT
Continued

1. Contact printer
2. Paper safe
3. Focusing magnifier
4. Cleaning aids:
   No Scratch Cleaner
   Kodak Film Cleaner
   Dust-Off Compressed Air Blower
   Anti-static brush
5. Contrast filters for Multigrade papers
6. Film-cassette opener

ISO RATINGS
Recently, the International Standards Organization established a new convention for designating film-speed ratings. Instead of the designation "ASA 400/27 DIN", for example, a film box will now state "ISO 400/27°". During a transition period, film boxes will display both the old and new rating conventions.

CLEANING AIDS

Air blowers

When you are making prints, every speck of dust adhering to the slide or negative will produce a noticeable spot on the print. The more you enlarge the print, the bigger the spot. The safest way to remove dust from slides and negatives is with an *air blower*. These are available in art supply stores and photo dealers and use disposable cartridges as their source of compressed air.

Anti-static brushes

When a static charge builds up on a piece of film, dust is attracted. To reduce the charge, as well as to remove dust particles – especially stubborn ones that will not blow away – you should have on hand an anti-static camel hair brush, which you lightly pass along the film's surface.

Film cleaners

To remove especially stubborn particles adhering to film, and to remove fingerprints and other spots, you should have available a commercial "film cleaner" – a solvent that you apply with a cotton swab.

Scratch-repair liquids

Occasionally, even with the best of care, a slide or negative may become scratched. A drop of No Scratch solution applied to the film may obscure the scratch and can be easily removed later with film cleaner.

CONTACT PRINTERS

In order to study the individual frames on a roll of negative film, you will need to purchase a single, positive print made from one exposure of the entire roll. To do this, you cut the film into strips, arrange them on top of a sheet of 8″ x 10″ printing paper, and expose this "sandwich" to light from your enlarger. *Contact printers* are designed to hold the strips of film motionless and flat against the paper while the exposure is being made. You can make your own contact printer by hinging a piece of glass to an 8½″ x 11″ (22 x 28 cm) or larger board by means of tape, or you can buy a commercially available version. The most expensive contact printer prints a space on which you can record comments or data next to each frame of film.

PAPER SAFES

Removing a single sheet of paper from the box-envelope combination in which paper is sold is time consuming and inconvenient. Therefore, you may wish to purchase a *paper safe* into which you can transfer as many sheets of paper as you wish. Some paper safes have shelves to accommodate more than one paper type at a time.

MULTIGRADE FILTERS

As will be explained in greater detail in Chapter Four, each time you make a black-and-white print you will need to decide on the "contrast grade" of paper to use. Once you have made your choice, you can either use that grade of paper to make the print, or you can use a "variable-contrast" paper, the grade of which is determined by the *Multigrade filter* you place in the enlarger's light path. There are seven filters in a complete set, and many sets include a convenient holder for mounting the filters below the enlarger lens. Or, you can use them in your enlarger's filter drawer. If your enlarger is fitted with a dichroic head, you can simply dial in the appropriate contrast filtration without the need to purchase a special set of filters.

FOCUSING AIDS

When correct focus is critical, you cannot rely on the naked eye. Special magnifiers are available that enable you to focus accurately. For maximum results, you must focus on a sheet of paper equal in thickness to the printing paper you will use.

FILM-CASSETTE OPENERS

Photographic dealers sell special film-cassette openers, but everyday bottle openers work perfectly well.

The sections of your darkroom where you use chemicals constitute your darkroom's "wet side". Items you should have on hand to outfit that side properly are discussed next.

WETSIDE EQUIPMENT

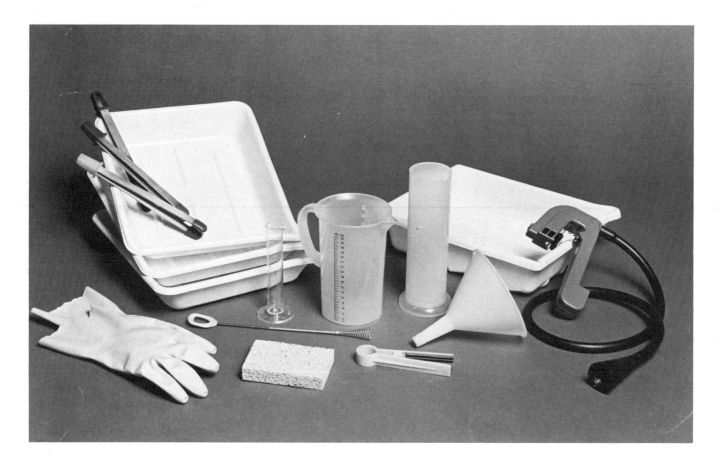

EQUIPMENT FOR THE DARKROOM WET SIDE
1. **Dishes and tongs**
2. **Rubber gloves**
3. **Selection of measures**
4. **Stirring rod**
5. **Sponge**
6. **Squeegee tongs for film**
7. **Funnel**
8. **Washing dish**
9. **Siphon and connecting hose**

TRAYS

Black-and-white prints are usually processed in flat, plastic dishes. You will need three normal dishes and one deep enough (4″ is usually sufficient) to allow a thorough wash of many prints at once. Be sure the dishes have ribs to prevent prints from adhering to the bottom of the dish. You can use 11″ x 14″ dishes for any print up to those dimensions, but if you process many prints smaller than 8″ x 10″, you will find that 5″ x 7″ dishes make more efficient use of your chemicals. (If you will be processing colour prints, you will also need a ''drum''. See page 116.)

GRADUATED MEASURES

Graduated measures are invaluable for mixing chemicals accurately. A small measure (2–4 oz) (59–118 ml) is useful for measuring small quantities; 16 oz (500 ml) beakers are handy for general use; and 32 oz (1 litre) and 64 oz (2 litres) beakers save you time when measuring large volumes. The measures most suitable for darkroom use are made of metal or plastic (glass breaks too easily). If you

buy plastic measures, avoid those constructed of hard, brittle plastic. Many beakers are made of a softer plastic that is much more durable.

STORAGE BOTTLES

Once mixed, chemicals deteriorate – some quickly, some slowly. If you are to derive the maximum shelf life from your chemicals, you must store them carefully. The two criteria for a good storage bottle are that it excludes light and that air can be removed from it. (Both light and air speed the breakdown of chemicals.) Any clean, opaque, squeezable plastic bottle found around the house will probably meet both criteria, although you can purchase expensive, commercially available versions, also. One type of specialized bottle, with sides that compress like an accordion, excludes light and air well but is difficult to clean because of the large surface area created by its pleats.

FUNNELS

Your darkroom benches will quickly become covered with puddles of chemicals unless you use funnels to transfer

GRADUATED MEASURES

Accurate measuring containers are indispensable in the darkroom. Small measures are necessary for small amounts of chemicals, while larger measures are useful for mixing chemicals in bulk. Containers made of plastic are safe for most darkroom work, but measures made of brittle plastic, which are slightly more accurate than ones made of pliable plastic, crack easily when dropped.

liquids from container to container. Buy at least two different sizes of funnel. The best funnels contain a fine-mesh screen designed to trap sediment and solid impurities floating in the chemicals.

STIRRING RODS

Shaking chemicals to mix them introduces oxygen and speeds their deterioration. The stirring rods sold by camera dealers are specifically designed for mixing darkroom chemicals. These rods permit deep and thorough agitation but do not disturb the surface and thereby introduce air.

THERMOMETERS

Careful control of temperature is critical in darkroom processing; therefore, it is essential that you own a high-quality thermometer. One versatile thermometer includes a clip for securing it to the lip of a dish or bottle. Metal-clad thermometers can also double as stirring rods.

TONGS

Darkroom chemicals can be caustic, so you do not want your fingers to come in contact with them. Moreover, you must be careful not to contaminate one chemical with another. You therefore need a separate set of tongs for each of the three processing dishes. Colour-coded tongs are less likely to be immersed accidentally in the wrong dish and contaminate a chemical or ruin a print.

STORAGE BOTTLES

A wide assortment of storage containers is available. Try to match the size of the bottles you purchase to the quantities of liquids that they will contain because most chemicals deteriorate in the presence of air.
The accordion-type bottle at right allows you to remove air by collapsing the bottle as the chemical is used up. Due to the large surface area of the accordion pleats, however, these bottles are difficult to wash and dry. You can remove air just as well from most soft plastic bottles simply by squeezing the sides before screwing on the cap.

Some manufacturers provide special areas on which you can jot down the contents of the bottle and other pertinent information.

EXPOSURE, PRINTING, AND PROCESSING AIDS

THE AUTOMATIC ENLARGER
Some modern enlargers are built with sophisticated electronics which automate many procedures that formerly relied on trial and error. Enlargers like the one above can be programmed to analyse the light being projected by the enlarger head and indicate the best paper grade to use and the correct exposure time.

In all likelihood, automatic enlargers will one day be as prevalent as automatic cameras are today. Nonetheless, because the first step in programming an automatic enlarger is to produce a correct print without its help, an automatic enlarger will never relieve you of the need to understand fundamental darkroom principles. Therefore, you must be proficient in traditional darkroom skills in order to use and adjust the automatic enlarger effectively.

TECHNOLOGICAL AIDS

Modern advances in technology offer a mixed blessing: routine procedures can be automated, but the danger always exists that by relying too much on technology before understanding fundamental principles, you become a slave to your equipment instead of its master.

The automated enlarger and enlarger meter described here can be of great help, but be sure you can work *without* them before you start with them.

The books shown are excellent resources that should be kept readily available in every darkroom.

ENLARGER METERS

Some hand-held exposure meters designed for use with a camera can also be adapted to measure the light projected by an enlarger. Meters with an enlarger attachment provide you with exposure information and also aid in selecting a paper grade.

Although enlarger attachments themselves are relatively inexpensive, only the more expensive meters accept such attachments. Therefore, if you are contemplating buying a hand-held meter anyway, you may want to consider one with an enlarger capability, but it makes little sense to purchase such a meter solely for darkroom use.

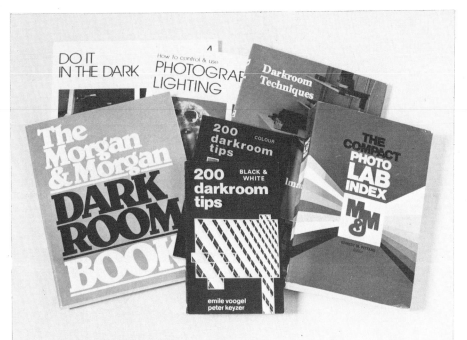

BOOKS

A good library of useful reference materials is a valuable darkroom resource. There is such a wide variety of films, papers, chemicals, and other supplies on the market that you will find the consolidated information in books far easier to refer to than the individual instruction sheets packaged with each product. In addition, some of the books such as the *Kodak Darkroom Data-guide* shown to the left, contain useful charts, diagrams, and even mechanical calculators to help you make decisions quickly and accurately.

Some books are sold through book- or camera stores, others you can obtain directly from the publisher.

DARKROOM ON A BUDGET

SAVING MONEY

Often you can save money by substituting inexpensive or home-made equipment for the manufactured items available through camera stores. If you substitute carefully, you will not in any way be compromising the quality of your results. Expensive darkroom aids can certainly make your task easier, but they do not necessarily make your prints better.

DARKROOM ON A BUDGET
1. **Brown juice bottles**
2. **Plastic cups marked with commonly used measurements**
3. **Coat hanger with clothes clips for turning coat hanger into a temporary negative drier**
4. **Small, plastic processing dishes**
5. **Bottle opener for opening film cassettes**
6. **Stopwatch with a sweep second hand**

PLASTIC TANK
An inexpensive plastic tank. It is capable of developing one roll of film and adapting to different film sizes. As mentioned earlier, plastic processing kits are most suitable if you process film only occasionally.

HOMEMADE CONTACT PRINTER
A piece of glass edged with tape and fastened to a cardboard or wooden base makes a useful contact printer.

2. THE DARKROOM

To the amateur photographer the term *darkroom* creates images of an elaborate and sophisticated arrangement of equipment – enlarger, sinks, dishes, bottles and shelves. In reality, modern processing equipment has made it possible for a darkroom to be quite simple. Now, the only irrevocable requirement for a darkroom is that it excludes light absolutely and that it provides the minimum amount of space necessary to accommodate an enlarger (and dishes, if the ability to make black-and-white prints is desired).

For example, since light-tight printing drums make it possible to execute the entire chemical segment of colour printing in normal light, you could set up your enlarger in a closet, load the drum there in darkness, and afterwards move to a kitchen or bathroom for processing. Even running water can be foregone within the darkroom, as long as it is available nearby. Similarly, you can process film by transferring it from the cassette into a "daylight" tank within a light-tight changing bag. Once the film is safely in the tank, you can perform all subsequent processing steps under normal light.

Of course, improvised darkrooms and darkrooms that meet only minimum requirements are hardly ideal. Nonetheless, if you have a good enlarger and discipline yourself to follow careful processing techniques, unorthodox surroundings will not prevent you from producing high-quality prints. Many famous photographers have been forced to perform their processing tasks in makeshift quarters, yet have produced results of unsurpassed quality. If necessary, you can too. Usually all it takes for you to fashion a comfortable, efficient, and entirely adequate darkroom right in your own home is a little imagination and a moderate amount of work.

This chapter presents some principles and suggestions for effective darkroom design. Obviously it will only be in a custom-built darkroom constructed from scratch that you will be able to incorporate all the principles and tips. However, if you spend time studying, visualizing, and planning your darkroom, as well as sketching a few possible layouts to scale on graph paper, you should be able to include many – if not all – the recommendations here. In the long run, the time and effort you spend planning your darkroom down to the finest detail will be rewarded by ease of movement and quality of photography.

PRINCIPLES OF DESIGN

SMALL DARKROOM DIAGRAM
Economy of motion is fundamental to efficient darkroom design. In addition, since you will be working in the dark much of the time, a well-planned darkroom will allow you to locate easily the materials you need without looking.

If possible, try to lay out your darkroom so that you always move in a single direction. In small darkrooms your motion will be basically circular. For example, while facing the enlarger in the design above, you would pick up the printing paper from your left, expose it, turn to your right to process it, turn again to your right to dry it, and turn yet another time to your right to trim the final print. The next turn would bring you back again to face the enlarger, where you would be set to repeat the process. By moving in such an orderly pattern, you will be less likely to lose your place in the middle of a process, and if you drop something in the dark, you will be able to find it easily.

LARGER DARKROOM DESIGN
In the best darkroom configuration, "dry" exposure operations are physically separated from "wet" processing operations. In larger darkrooms, the operations can be performed along opposite walls, although you must still be careful to lay out an efficient and logical sequence of movements.

The layout at right is adaptable to smaller or larger areas than shown. The advantage of long, wide benches and sinks is that they can accommodate oversize prints or special procedures that involve extra dishes (e.g. printing for permanence, p. 78).

The darkroom shown uses a walk-in, light-trap entrance cubicle, painted black, instead of a light-tight door. Heavy dark curtains (symbolized by the two wavy lines) permit you to enter or leave the darkroom without admitting light. This method is especially convenient if more than one person will be needing access to the darkroom at one time.

LIGHTPROOF VENT
You will need a means for admitting fresh air into your darkroom which will provide the necessary ventilation without admitting light. To construct a lightproof vent:
1. *Cut hole* at least 1′ (30 cm) square in a door, wall, or window.
2. *Cover opening* on the outside with wire screening or slats.
3. *Surround inside borders* of the hole with wood strips that protrude 1″ (3 cm) into the darkroom.
4. *Cut cover* for the vent from Masonite or plywood. Make the cover at least 4″ (10 cm) wider than the hole in both dimensions.
5. *Attach strips of wood* along any two opposite edges of the cover. The strips should protrude $1\frac{7}{8}$″ (5 cm) from the surface of the cover.
6. *Attach additional strips of wood* along the remaining two edges of the cover. These strips should protrude only 1″ from the surface of the cover.
7. *Paint inside of cover* flat black.
8. *Affix cover* over the hole so that the wood strips on the cover encompass the wood strips surrounding the hole. Because of the two narrower wood strips on the cover, air will be able to flow through the trap, but light will not (see diagram).

Size

Big is not necessarily best. Unless you want to make huge enlargements, a 6′ x 8′ (1.8 x 2.4 m) floor space will be adequate, comfortable, and efficient. Even with benches built on three sides, an area this size will still allow you to have 30″ to 36″ (76.2 to 91.4 cm) of aisle space. If you forego a sink and also decide to use stackable dishes, your darkroom could occupy as little as 3′ x 4′ (.91 x 1.2 m).

Light exclusion

Try to select a space with only one door and no windows. If windows are present, cover them with enough lightproof fabric or wood to block all light from entering. Caulk any room or window seams that admit light.

To block light from slipping around your darkroom door, construct a light baffle around the door's edges by attaching wood strips to the door *frame* in such a way that the strips overlap the door by about 1″. To block light from entering under the door, staple a folded piece of fabric along the door's bottom edge. Adjust the size and placement of the fabric so that it makes good contact with the floor but does not bind when the door is opened and closed. Finish the job by adding a lock or latch to the door to prevent visitors from entering at the wrong time.

When you think you have blocked all leaks, stand in the room for 10 minutes with the light out to accustom your eyes to the darkness, then carefully inspect every surface and seam for evidence of stray light.

Dry and wet areas

In a thoughtfully designed darkroom, there is a distinct separation of "dry" areas from "wet" areas. In the dry areas you perform all procedures that do not involve chemicals or water: film loading, paper loading, and enlarging. In the wet areas you perform procedures that do involve chemicals or water: developing and washing. By creating distinct dry and wet sections in your darkroom, you minimize the likelihood of accidentally ruining a procedure by allowing chemicals or water to come in contact with items that should remain dry.

If your darkroom design includes only one bench, build a small partition to prevent liquids from running from the wet section onto the dry section.

Flow

Since you will be performing many procedures in total darkness, a good design will provide for a logical, efficient flow of motion as you progress from one procedure to the next. In a darkroom with benches on three sides, plan for a clockwise or counterclockwise progression. In a small darkroom with only one bench, the sequence should go from left to right or right to left.

Ventilation

You can improvise a rudimentary ventilation system by drilling a section of holes near the ceiling and another near the floor. To obstruct light, build a light trap over each section (see illustration). For more effective ventilation, a special electric fan that contains built-in light blocks can be purchased.

Plumbing

The ideal is to have running water available right in your darkroom. If you are converting a spare bathroom, you may be able to use the sink already present; if at all possible, however, substitute a larger sink designed especially for darkroom use.

COIN SAFELIGHT TEST
To double-check the reliability of your safelight, you can perform this simple test. Place a coin on top of a piece of unexposed enlarging paper that is positioned face up in the area of brightest safelight illumination in your darkroom. Allow the coin to sit for about 5 minutes, then process the paper normally. If the outline of the coin is at all apparent, then your safelight is too strong. Check the bulb, the filtration, and the distance of the light from the paper. Make adjustments and repeat the test until no outline is left on the paper.

Safelights

Many photographic papers can be viewed without harm under a safelight of the proper colour. Locate a socket for your safelight, which should be built at least 4′ (1.2 m) above the darkroom benches in a position where the illumination will not fall directly on your enlarger masking frame. (Direct light falling on the masking frame makes it difficult to focus and work with the projected image.

Be careful to locate the safelight switch in a place where it cannot possibly be confused with the switch for the standard room light.

One way to obtain the most illumination from the least amount of safelight wattage is to paint the inside of the darkroom white. (As long as your basic darkroom construction is light-tight, there is no need to paint the walls black.)

DESIGN REFINEMENTS

**ADJUSTABLE ENLARGER
BASEBOARD**
If you frequently need to produce
enlargements exceeding the capacity of your
enlarger, you can remount the enlarger
column onto a customised bench that allows
adjustments in the height of the baseboard.

The diagram above shows how the
enlarger image (dotted line) becomes
progressively larger as the baseboard is
lowered to the floor. Wooden slats support
the baseboard at various intermediate levels
of enlargements. When constructing such a
device, be sure to cut the top opening large
enough so that it does not interfere with the
image formed at the lower baseboard level.
The distance from the enlarger to the bottom
level will have to exceed 3 ft (.9 m) to produce
a 20″ x 24″ (51 x 61 cm) print from a 35mm
negative.

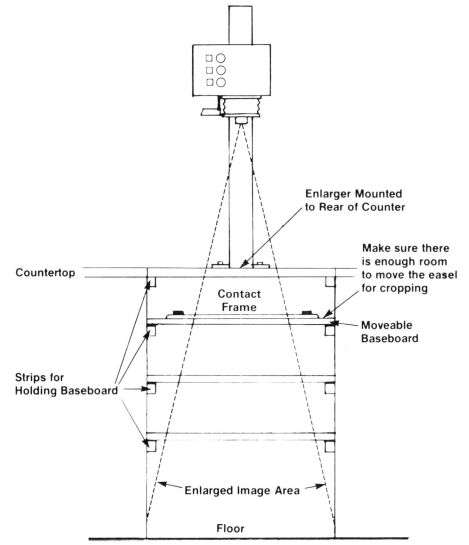

Enlarger Mounted
to Rear of Counter

Make sure there
is enough room
to move the easel
for cropping

Countertop

Contact
Frame

Moveable
Baseboard

Strips for
Holding Baseboard

Enlarged Image Area

Floor

Once you have decided on a location
for your darkroom, established its floor
plan, arranged for any plumbing and
electrical work that will be needed, and
determined a logical plan for movement,
you can refine your design for maximum
efficiency and utilization of space.

ENLARGER MOUNTS

In a standard darkroom set-up the enlarger is mounted on a bench, and the
size to which photographs can be enlarged is limited by how high above the
bench you can raise the enlarger head. A
more versatile alternative is to mount the
column along which the enlarger head

travels directly onto the benchtop rather
than onto a baseboard, as is normally
done.

If you construct the benchtop so that
you can lower the portion that serves as
the enlarger's baseboard, you will then
be able to make extreme enlargements.
Take care when constructing such an
apparatus to make certain that the adjustable portion of the bench remains completely parallel to the film plane in all
positions; otherwise, the projected image
will become distorted, and focusing will
be difficult or impossible. Also, to make
certain that the enlarger head will not
vibrate and thus blur the image, securely
brace the top of the column to the wall
with wire.

ENLARGER ACCESSORIES

Try to locate all enlarger controls and tools as close to the enlarger as possible. If space is at a premium, mount a pegboard on the wall behind the enlarger to accommodate dodging tools, filters, and other accessories. An excellent location for paper storage is under the bench and near the enlarger, in drawers or on shelves. If you have room, you can locate a paper safe close-by.

MISCELLANEOUS ACCESSORIES

Changing bag

Even though you have taken great care to make your darkroom light-tight, you may wish to store a changing bag near the dry area of your darkroom. Then, if something goes wrong while you are loading film in the dark, you can quickly transfer the film to the changing bag and turn on the lights to deal with the problem.

Additional light

In order to evaluate your results while your prints are still in the fixer, you may want to mount a normal light above the fixer dish.

Study area

If sufficient bench space is available, you may wish to arrange a final prep-and-study area at one end of your darkroom. It would contain a light box for viewing negatives and slides as well as equipment for cutting and mounting prints and maintaining records.

BUILDING YOUR OWN FIBREGLASS SINK
You can easily and inexpensively make a sink of the exact dimensions you need out of fibreglass. The first step is to construct a wood frame with a plywood bottom that slants toward the drain end of the sink. Be sure to seal all joints in the sink with plastic filler. To cover the frame with fibreglass, you will need polyester resin, fibreglass cloth, a mixing bucket, and one or more paint brushes with which to apply the mixed resin. Work in a well-ventilated area using brushes you can throw away afterwards. To cover the wooden frame with fibreglass:

1. *Cut Fibreglass cloth* to fit the frame.
2. *Set cloth aside.*
3. *Mix enough resin* to coat the inside of the frame.
4. *Brush resin on all surfaces* that will later be covered with the fibreglass cloth.
5. *Position cloth* over the wet frame. (Note: Work fast. The resin dries very quickly.)
6. *Smooth cloth* over the form and allow to dry for 15 minutes.
7. *Mix enough resin* to cover the cloth.
8. *Apply a coat of resin* over the Fibreglass.
9. *Apply resin to dry, then repeat previous step.*
10. When the fibreglass is thoroughly dry, *cut a drain opening* in lower end and install drain plumbing.

The completely finished sink is shown on the next page.

A MODEL DARKROOM

Enlarger

Safelight

Color-Processing Equipment (Drums)

Safelig

Colour Analyser

Timer

Paper Storage

Dish Storage

Trimming A

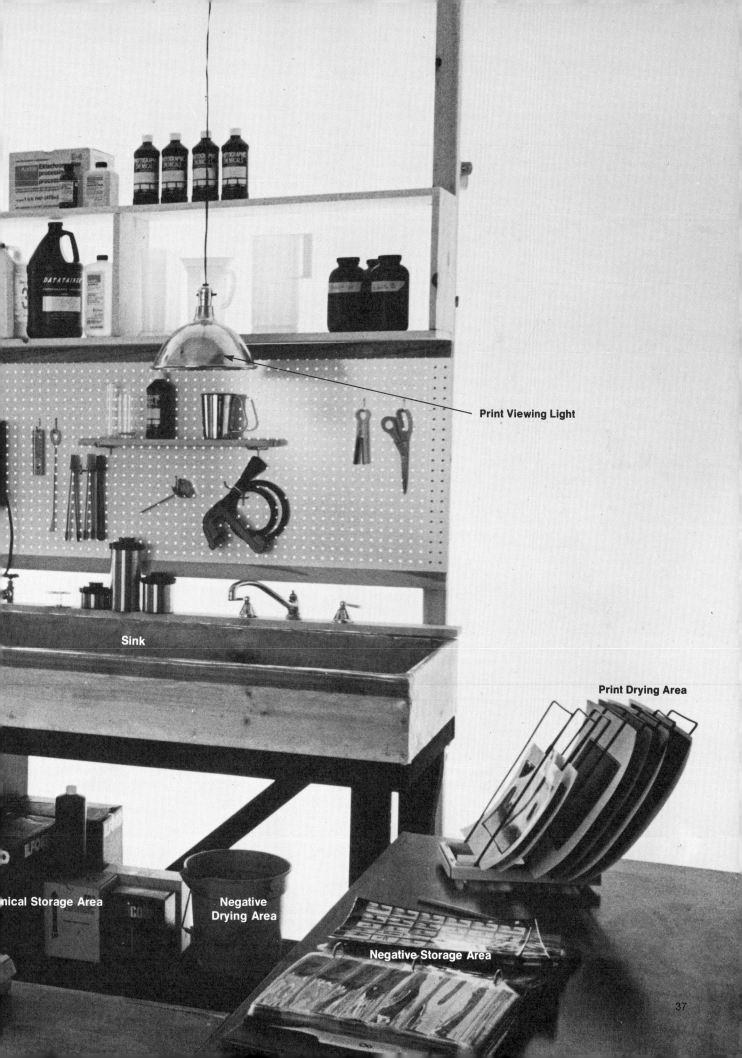

Print Viewing Light

Sink

Print Drying Area

...nical Storage Area

Negative
Drying Area

Negative Storage Area

3. THE BLACK-AND-WHITE NEGATIVE

**MATERIALS FOR PROCESSING
BLACK AND WHITE FILM**
Processing black and white film requires
very little space, a minimum of equipment,
and only a small amount of time. The
chemicals and equipment pictured above are
sufficient to process completely a roll of film.

The *Negative* lies at the very heart of black and white processing. Although techniques exist to help "rescue" a deficient negative, the more adept you are at producing high-quality negatives, the more successful you will be in the darkroom.

The manufacturers of darkroom equipment and supplies have a vested interest in your success and therefore make their products as foolproof as possible. On most occasions, you will obtain excellent negatives, simply by following the manufacturer's instructions carefully. However, you must not consider their recommendations to be infallible; you must be prepared to deviate from normal procedures when you feel that circumstances so dictate.

As your skills improve, you will no doubt want to try to exert some creative control over the images you produce in the darkroom. By all means experiment, but be cautious. Initially, at least, try to deviate from standard procedures only when you have a specific goal in mind, such as adjusting contrast. Then evaluate your results by how closely you came to reaching your goal. Otherwise, the results of your experiments are likely to be difficult to interpret and hard to reproduce.

As you become adept in the darkroom, you will begin to realize that you cannot divorce the *taking* of a photograph from the *processing* of it. The two either complement or interfere with each other. Once you understand how to use this inter-relationship to best advantage, you will be on the road to achieving your full potential as a photographer.

Tone. *A tone* in a black and white photograph is a shade of grey. Any two shades of grey that are distinguishable represent two different tones. Almost every scene you photograph will contain a range of tones, as will every negative. Since the human eye can perceive a broader range of tones than can be recorded on film, you must learn to recognize when the range of tones in a scene exceeds your film's ability to record them, and then how to compensate in the darkroom (p. 54).

Since light meters respond to tonal differences, you can use a light meter to measure the tonal range of a scene. The technique is to hold your meter (either a meter built into your camera or a hand-held one) close to the darkest and then the lightest tones in a scene. The difference between the readings you obtain from the two tones represents the *range* of tones contained in the scene.

Try to become an expert at evaluating tones by eye, even though the most accurate method will always be to use a meter. In most circumstances, being able to approximate the tonal range of a scene or negative will be sufficient for your needs.

CHARACTERISTICS OF FILM

PEBBLES
The best darkroom results are obtained when you match a thorough understanding of films with just as thorough an understanding of darkroom chemicals and processes. The photograph above was taken on a fine-grained film which was then under-developed slightly to lower contrast and provide a very sharp print.

How film works

The basis of contemporary photography involves the effect of light on a class of chemicals known as silver halides. These compounds display the unusual characteristic of turning black after being exposed to light and chemical processing.

The production of a stable image on film involves three primary steps: first, an emulsion of silver halide crystals suspended in gelatin and mounted on a firm but flexible triacetate base, the film, is *exposed* by allowing light to strike it and form a *latent* (undeveloped) *image*; second, the latent image is *developed* by means of specially formulated chemicals; and third, the developed image is *fixed* by

means of additional chemicals which remove the silver halide crystals that were not struck by light in the first step. The end result is called a *negative* because every dark point on the film corresponds to a light area in the original scene, and every light point on the film corresponds to a dark area in the original scene.

Grain structure

The size of the metallic silver crystals contained in the emulsion layer of a processed film produces what is referred to as the film's *grain structure*. The larger the size of each crystal, the more noticeable it is. In large-grained films, clusters of developed silver crystals are readily apparent to the naked eye.

Resolving power

The ability of a film to show a distinct separation between two closely spaced lines within the same shade of grey is called its *resolving power*. In practical terms, the greater a film's resolving power, the sharper the image it will form. Grain and resolving power are directly related: the smaller the grain, the greater

the resolving power and the sharper the image.

Sensitivity to light

Films are produced with varying degrees of sensitivity to light. The higher a film's *speed*, as designated by its ASA/ISO rating, the more sensitive it is to light. Moreover, hand in hand with film speed is film grain. The faster a film, or the higher its ASA/ISO rating, the larger the film's grain structure.

The ASA/ISO numbers are carefully calculated to facilitate film-speed comparisons. Thus, ASA/ISO50 film responds twice as quickly to light as does ASA/ISO25 film, but one-quarter as quickly as ASA/ISO200 film.

The rating assigned to a particular film by its manufacturer assumes that the film will be processed "normally". By changing development times, or by using special developers, you can use the film as if it has an effective speed different from its ASA/ISO rating.

Colour sensitivity

Films that respond equally to all colours in the spectrum are called *panchromatic*.

Some special-purpose films are *ortho-chromatic*; that is, they respond normally to blue and green, but red comes out black in a print made from their negatives. *Infra-red* film responds to light waves beyond the range of the visible spectrum. The often unpredictable results that are obtained with infra-red film are sometimes used creatively to add novelty to an otherwise dull scene.

Choosing a film

Because of the differences in grain structure and resolving power among films of different speed ratings, your selection of film must strike a balance between the amount of light in a scene and the amount of grain and resolving power you need or want. Although there are darkroom techniques that will increase the amount of grain shown by a developed negative, there is no way to improve upon a film's inherent grain structure. However, one of the advantages of processing your own film is that once you learn the applicable techniques, you will be able to exercise a substantial amount of control over the final appearance of the image on your negative, even if the film is exposed under less than ideal conditions which result in a loss of detail in the negative and an increase in grain size.

Negative density

The result of developing film is a build-up of metallic silver on the negative in proportion to the amount of light that originally struck the film. The greater the build-up, the denser the negative is said to be. A properly exposed, properly developed negative is "optimally" dense. Over-exposure of the film in the camera or over-development in the dark-room produces too much density, due to abnormally heavy concentrations of metallic silver. Under-exposure or under-development causes reduced density and a loss in highlight detail. Optimal negative density, therefore, is important for producing high-quality prints.

Negative contrast

Reproduction of images in black and white photography depends on the contrast between different shades of grey. Negatives that contain many slightly different shades of grey between the extremes of black and white are referred to as having *low contrast*. Negatives that show few, and more obvious, gradations of grey are referred to as having *high contrast*.

COMMON BLACK AND WHITE FILMS

Film	ASA/ ISO	Grain* (C M F VF)	Characteristics
KODAK			
Panatomic-X	32	VF +	Useful where excellent sharpness (resolution) is necessary and slow speed is no drawback
Plus-X	125	VF	Excellent general-purpose film with wide latitude and medium speed
Tri-X	400	F	Good general-purpose film when shooting is mostly in low-light situations; speed can be pushed
Royal-X pan	1250	C	Useful for extremely low-light situations
High Contrast Copy 5069	64		For making copies of b/w negatives; no grey tones
ILFORD			
Pan F	50	VF +	Useful where excellent sharpness is necessary and slow speed is no drawback
FP-4	125	VF	Excellent general-purpose film with wide latitude and medium speed
HP-5	400	F	Good general-purpose film when shooting is mostly in low-light situations; speed can be pushed
HP-5 Autowinder	400	F	72 exposure cassettes
XP-1	400	VF	Chromogenic film
AGFA			
Agfapan 25	25	VF +	For extreme sharpness
Agfapan 100	100	VF	General-purpose film
Agfapan 400 Professional	400	F	Useful for low-light situations
Agfa Vario-XL	50–1600		Chromogenic film
Agfa DiaDirect	32		For b/w slides from transparencies

*C–coarse, M–medium, F–fine, VF–very fine

CHEMISTRY AND EQUIPMENT

**EQUIPMENT FOR PROCESSING
BLACK AND WHITE NEGATIVES**
1. **Funnel**
2. **Storage bottles**
3. **Graduated measure for mixing and
   pouring**
4. **Thermometer**
5. **Processing tank and reel**
6. **Washing hose (optional)**
7. **Squeegee**
8. **Stopwatch or timer**
9. **Clips for hanging negatives**
10. **Film-cassette opener**
11. **Scissors**
12. **Film**

CHEMISTRY

The only chemicals you really need to develop films are a developer, a fixer, and some water. Additional chemicals and steps – stop bath, hypo clearing agent, and wetting agent – are optional refinements designed to save you time as well as to extend the life of your chemicals and film. The various chemicals you will be using are discussed below in the order that you will need them.

Developer

The developer converts exposed silver halide crystals into metallic silver, which produces the blacks and greys characteristic of black and white photography. Of all the chemicals involved in processing film, none is more important than the developer. Each developer has its own strengths and weaknesses, and each performs best under a particular set of circumstances. The developer you select will determine your film's effective speed, as well as your negative's grain and resolution. Moreover, you must match both the developer and the developing time to the conditions under which the film was exposed in order to achieve optimal negative density and contrast.

Stop bath

Once development is completed, you must remove the developer from the film's surface in order to prevent over-development of the film and contamination of chemicals in later steps. One way to halt development is to use water, filling and emptying the tank twice within 30 seconds. Or, you can use a special stop bath which acts on the developer more quickly and more thoroughly than water alone.

The stop bath procedure is simple: you replace the developer in the tank with the stop bath solution, agitate for 15 seconds, and then discard the stop bath. (An indicator-stop bath solution can be re-used until a change in colour signals that the solution is exhausted.)

Fixer

If you were to remove film from the developing tank immediately after the stop bath step, the negatives would appear "fogged" because of the remaining silver halide crystals which were not originally exposed to light and therefore were not converted to metallic silver by the developer. The fixer step dissolves these unexposed crystals, thereby removing the fog and making the film no longer light sensitive.

Fixing time varies between 2 minutes and 10 minutes depending on the type of fixer you are using. A rapid fixer will work in 2–4 minutes, while a regular fixer requires 5–10 minutes. Fixing time is also affected by how fresh the solution is. The older it is, the more time you must allow for the fixer to do its work.

Fixing time is somewhat arbitrary, but standard practice is to leave film in the fixer twice as long as is necessary to clear all visible fog. Should you find your film still fogged after removing it from the fixer, your fixer is either depleted or contaminated. To remedy the problem, you can fix the film again using fresh chemicals.

Hypo clearing agent

Any chemicals remaining on the film after processing is completed will continue to act and eventually will stain, fade, or completely destroy the photographic image. A thorough washing for 30 minutes under running water will usually eliminate chemical residues, but you can speed up the process and make it more reliable by inserting a wash with *hypo clearing agent* between two short water washes. Using a hypo clearing agent shortens the total wash time to 3–8 minutes.

Wetting agent

Due to normal surface tension, water forms beads on the surface of film. When the beads dry, minerals are deposited on the film and appear as spots. Solutions known as *wetting agents* prevent beads of water from forming by reducing surface tension so the water flows off the film more smoothly. Normal procedure involves soaking the film briefly in a wetting agent, such as Photo Technology 326, before hanging the film up to dry. (If you use a squeegee or sponge to remove excess liquid from the film before hanging it up, first moisten the squeegee or sponge with a wetting agent to minimize tye likelihood of scratching the film's delicate emulsion layer.)

A complete set of chemicals for black and white processing consisting of three types of developer, two types of hypo, a stop bath, a wetting agent and a solution for quick washing.

A film dryer with a heater and fan which takes up a minimum of room and the plastic section can be folded for storage as shown in the base of the photograph.

THE BLACK-AND-WHITE DEVELOPER

Black and White Developers

Developer	Film speed increase (S—slight; N—Normal; H—high; VH—very high; D—decrease)	Chemical form (P—powder; L—liquid concentrate)	Grain (M—medium; F—fine; VF—very fine)	Dilution	Can be replenished and re-used	Speed of development (S—slow; N—normal; F—fast; VH—very fast)	Characteristics
AGFA							
Rodinal	N	L	M	1:25	No	N	High acutance developer
Atomal	H	P	VF	1:1	No	S	Very fine grain PQ developer
ILFORD							
ID11	N	P	M	1:1	Yes	N	Ideal general-purpose developer similar to D76
Microphen	H	P	F	1:1	Yes	N	Good for uprated exposure work
Perceptol	D	L	VF	1:1	Yes	S	Ideal for over-exposed film
Ilfosol	N	L	F	1:1	No	F	General purpose one-shot developer
XP-1	N	L	VF	1:1	No	N	Only for XP-1 chromogenic film
PHOTO TECHNOLOGY							
Unitol	N	L	F	1:5	No	N	Useful for push processing
Definol	N	L	VF	1:20	No	S	Maximum definition with medium speed films
KODAK							
D76	N–H	P	F	1:1	Yes	N	One of the best general use developers
Microdol-X	N	P	VF	1:3	Yes	S	Very fine grain developer for producing extra sharp negatives; for best results use diluted
HC 110	N	L	M–F	Varies	No	S–F	General-purpose liquid; speed of developer depends on dilution
Universal	N	L	M	1:4	No	F	Can be used to develop paper as well as film
DK-50	N	P	M	1:1	Yes	N–F	General-purpose developer
PATERSON							
Acuspeed	H–VH	L	F	1:1	No	VF	Gives maximum possible increase of speed
Aculux	H–VH	L	F	1:5	No	N	For good tonal gradation
Acuspecial	VH	P	M–F	None	No	N	Good definition with fine grain
TETENAL							
Neofin Blue	N	L	F	500cc phial	No	N	For slow speed films
Neofin Red	N	L	F	500cc phial	No	N	For medium speed films
Leicanol	N	L	VF	1:1	N0	S	Compensating developer – ideal for flash work

Significant differences exist among the various groups of developers: some work best for preserving the grain structure of fine-grained films, some are recommended for use only with properly exposed film, some are used to "push" under-exposed film, some are most effective for increasing negative contrast, and some are best for decreasing negative density. In all likelihood your personal style of photography will cause you to find that most of your film can best be processed using one or two particular developers. Your strategy should be to identify your preferred developers, then master their use so completely that they become a standard against which you compare all others.

Black-and-white film processing is subject to a large number of variables. Although manufacturers offer guidelines for use of their products, no matter which developer you choose, you will need to experiment with time, temperature, and exposure.

Here are descriptions of different types of developers and some discussions on important aspects of developer selection. Find the category of developer that seems most likely to meet your needs, select a brand from that category, then completely familiarize yourself with that specific developer. Later you can experiment with other developers as your needs and desires indicate.

General developers

Most people find a good general-purpose developer such as Kodak D76 or Ilford ID11 to be the mainstay of their darkrooms. General-purpose developers are proven formulae which produce negatives of normal contrast, reasonably fine grain, good overall sharpness and proper density, using average development times. If necessary, you can use these developers occasionally to "push" under-exposed films with acceptable results.

Fine-grain developers

If your regular practice is to shoot very slow film in order to obtain sharp, fine-grained negatives suitable for large blow-ups, then fine-grain developers such as Kodak Microdol-X, Ilford Perceptol, and Paterson Acuspecial will serve you well, as long as you do not mind the increased development times they require.

Veratile developers

If you shoot in a wide variety of situations – pushing fast film to its ASA/ISO limit one day and making fine-grained 16″ x 20″ (41 x 51 cm) blow-ups the next – consider using a versatile developer such as Photo Technology's Unitol, or Ilford Microphen. These products can accommodate a wide range of film speeds and contrasts. With practice, you can use these developers to obtain quality results over a broad range of conditions.

Contrast developers

Sometimes you may want to use your developer to increase contrast, for example, when a roll of film has been shot outside on an overcast day or when you want to photograph line drawings (such as diagrams and sketches). Contrast developers such as Kodak D19 accomplish this by rendering all tones as either pure black or pure white.

Compensating developers

Each type of film responds to a limited range of tones. If the range of tones in a scene exceeds the range of tones your film is able to record, detail will be lost in the shadows and highlights of the photographic image. If you have exposed a roll of film under conditions such that you know the scene exceeded your film's tonal range, you can use a compensating developer to retain more of the highlight and shadow detail than would be possible using a standard developer. Examples of good compensating developers include Acufine ACU-1 and Universal.

Dilution vs. replenishment

Each time you process a roll of film, the strength of the chemicals in your developer becomes somewhat depleted. Developers intended for disposal after one use are diluted with water before being used. Developers intended for reuse are used full strength, then replenished by the addition of more of the concentrate or of a special replenishment solution.

Disposable developers will yield better negatives with greater consistency than will re-usable developers, but their processing times are longer. Unless short development times are very important to you, however, the quality and consistency you can achieve with disposable developers are worth the few minutes of additional processing time.

Shelf life

Every manufacturer specifies his product's shelf life, that is, the period of time after mixing during which the chemicals should continue to yield satisfactory results. Because the principal cause of chemical deterioration is interaction with oxygen (oxidation), the advertised shelf life of a chemical is attainable only if nearly all oxygen is removed from the storage container. You should store mixed chemicals in airtight plastic bottles that you squeeze firmly to force out extra air before capping. Most developers stored in this manner will keep for three to six months.

Development time

The degree of density to which a latent image is developed depends upon the strength and temperature of the developer, the amount of time during which the developer is allowed to act, and the amount of agitation applied to the developing tank. Manufacturers of developers and film usually enclose general instructions and time-temperature charts with their products; you can also consult a book of photographic tables and formulae to obtain this information. However, since the optical elements in your particular enlarger may affect contrast, you may need to experiment with increased or decreased development times in order to achieve the contrast quality you desire. (Condenser enlargers often require shorter development times, diffusion enlargers often require longer development times.) Be sure you understand the technique for proper agitation (p. 47) before you attempt to develop a roll of film.

Development times in minutes for various films in Kodak D76 diluted 1:1 or Ilford ID11

	TEMPERATURE				
	18°C/65°F	20°C/68°F	21°C/70°F	22°/72°F	24°C/75°F
Kodak					
Panatomic-X	8	7	$6\frac{1}{2}$	$5\frac{3}{4}$	5
Plus-X	$8\frac{1}{2}$	$7\frac{1}{4}$	$6\frac{3}{4}$	6	$5\frac{1}{4}$
Tri-X	$11\frac{1}{2}$	10	$9\frac{1}{4}$	$8\frac{1}{2}$	$7\frac{1}{4}$
Ilford					
Pan-F	$10\frac{1}{2}$	9	8	7	6
FP-4	$10\frac{1}{2}$	9	8	7	6
HP-5	14	12	$11\frac{1}{2}$	$9\frac{3}{4}$	8

LOADING FILM

→ 34A   → 35   → 35A   → 36   → 36.

LOADING FILM ONTO A METAL REEL

1. *Grasp reel* in your left hand.
2. *Check with left index finger* to make certain that the outer ends of the spiral wires that make up the reel point toward the film.
3. *Bow film* slightly by squeezing its edges between the fingertips of your right hand.
4. *Insert end of film* into the slot in the axle of the reel.
5. *Hold film in slot* with pressure from your left index finger.

6. *Place thumb and index finger* of your right hand against the edges of the reel. (Maintain a bow in the film.)
7. *Rotate reel counterclockwise* with your *left* hand. Allow the film to slide through your right thumb and finger against the reel.

8. *Continue rotating reel,* making certain the film feeds straight onto the reel and no kinks form, until all the film is loaded.
9. *Cut film spool* from the end of the roll (or detach the spool by removing the tape).
10. *Insert reel in tank.*
11. *Cover tank.*

DEVELOPING REELS

In order to ensure that all parts of a roll of film are evenly immersed in the processing chemicals, you must roll your film onto processing reels designed so that the film's surfaces can be freely reached by the various chemicals involved. Since film incorrectly loaded on a reel usually develops unevenly (as happened to the film in the photographs at the top of this page), you should practise loading with an expendable roll of film until you have mastered the technique. Otherwise, you will be likely to ruin part or all of the first few rolls of film you try to develop.

Loading metal reels

You can learn to load plastic reels easily by following the directions included with the reel. In order to learn to load a metal

reel, you will need either an already developed roll of film or an unexposed roll to "sacrifice" for the sake of education. There are two secrets to loading film onto a metal reel: (1) you must "bow" the film the proper amount by squeezing its edges between your fingertips as you feed it onto the reel and (2) you must not allow the film to feed onto the reel at an angle. The photograph (top left) shows a reel being loaded improperly. The film is not being fed straight onto the reel, which will result in crushed film and uneven development.

The photographs above illustrate how to load film onto a metal reel. If you are left-handed, reverse the references to right and left hands, and rotate the reel clockwise instead of anticlockwise. Practise first while looking at the reel, then practise in total darkness.

AGITATION TECHNIQUE

By keeping the chemical solution in motion, agitation replenishes depleted chemicals, resulting in even development and normal contrast (middle photograph at right).

Effects of improper agitation

Insufficient agitation allows depleted chemicals to cling to the surface of the film, preventing full development and causing contrast to be too low (top photograph). *Too much agitation* causes chemical reactions to take place too quickly, resulting in excessive density in the negatives and an increase in contrast (bottom photograph at right). Also, over vigorous agitation causes developer to surge through the film's sprocket holes, producing *surge marks* along the edge of the film.

Proper agitation technique

The agitation procedure described here will produce excellent results under most circumstances; however, always consult the manufacturer's instructions to determine if a special technique is recommended. (Note: Where air bubbles cling to the surface of the film, chemicals cannot approach close enough to the film for a chemical reaction to occur. By tapping the tank once or twice on a hard surface immediately after you pour a processing chemical into the tank, you will dislodge any air bubbles. Thereafter, follow the normal agitation procedure.)

Procedure

Unless the film's manufacturer recommends otherwise, firmly but gently turn the developing tank over and back each time an agitation step is called for. Practise for a few moments without film and with plain water in the tank until you have developed a smooth agitation rhythm. The over-and-back sequence should take about 2 seconds to complete.

No agitation

Correct agitation

Excessive agitation

DEVELOPING BLACK-AND-WHITE FILM STEP-BY-STEP

WHAT DO YOU NEED?

1. **Photographic thermometer,** *for determining the temperature of the chemicals you are using*
2. **Squeegee tongs,** *for removing excess water from film before hanging it to dry*
3. **Bottle opener,** *for opening film cassettes*
4. **Scissors,** *for snipping the ends of film*
5. **Clips,** *for hanging film while it dries*
6. **Reels,** *for holding film while processing takes place*
7. **Tank,** *for submerging film in chemicals within a light-free environment*
8. **Jug,** *for pouring chemicals*
9. **Developer and fixer,** *chemicals necessary for developing film and removing unexposed silver*
10. **Stop bath,** *optional but very useful solution used to halt action of developer thoroughly*
11. **Hypo clearing bath,** *optional but very useful chemical used to move fixer from film*
12. **Wetting agent,** *used to reduce surface tension of water to promote spotless drying*
13. **Timer,** *to measure accurately the duration of processing steps*

GENERAL INSTRUCTIONS

Determining development time

Packaged with each roll of black and white film you will find an information sheet that tells you how long to leave the film in the developer. All you need to do is measure the temperature of your chemicals, then look up the appropriate developing time for the type of developer you are using. Be sure that all your chemicals, including your wash water, are within about 3°C (5°F) of each other. The times required for chemicals other than the developer are listed on the bottles they come in or on separate instruction sheets.

Agitation

When you are performing an agitation step as part of an actual development sequence, for the first 15 seconds you should agitate continuously. Thereafter, you should agitate for only the last 5 seconds (i.e. for two complete tank inversions) of each 30-second period. At the end of the final 30 second period, do not agitate.

Using multi-reel tanks

Tanks which hold two reels can be handled in the same manner as single-reel tanks, but tanks which hold three or more reels should be agitated every 60 seconds instead of every 30 seconds. If you want to develop a single roll of film in a multi-reel tank, be sure to fill the extra space in the tank with empty reels, and fill the tank completely with chemicals.

Mixing chemicals

Many darkroom chemicals must be mixed together or diluted before they can be used to process film. Consult the appendix for instructions on how to mix chemicals before you start to process a reel of film.

Pouring chemicals

Pour chemicals quickly and smoothly. Once a chemical is poured into the developing tank, be sure to tap the tank a few times on a hard surface to dislodge any air bubbles that may be clinging to the film. Start pouring chemicals out of the tank early enough so the tank is completely drained by the time the step should be completed.

Chemical depletion

If you are using a re-usable chemical, you need to know when to replenish or discard it. To keep track of how many times a solution has been used, you can make a small tick mark after each use on a piece of tape stuck onto the storage container.

Timing individual steps

The standard technique for timing individual steps is to start the timer at the same time you begin to pour a chemical into the tank. An alternative method, which is optional with small tanks but mandatory with large tanks (holding three or more reels) is to pour the developer into the tank *before* you turn the lights out to load the film into the reel. In this manner, when you place the loaded reel in the development tank, all of the film begins the development process at the same time. For subsequent steps, you should prepare a spare tank with the next chemical needed, so that when you turn the lights off and remove the first tank's cover, you will only need to transfer the reel from the empty tank to the full one.

Opening the tank
Do not expose the film to light until after the film is fixed. Use the light-tight top on your tank for both pouring chemicals into the tank and pouring them out again.

Chemical contamination
It is surprisingly easy to contaminate one chemical with another. To prevent contamination, be sure your developing tank and reels are spotlessly clean and dry before you start to develop a roll of film; rinse your measures with water between uses; develop the habit of rinsing off your thermometer with water each time after you have immersed it in a chemical; always return chemicals to their proper bottles immediately after use; and clean up spilled chemicals promptly.

Organization
Assemble everything in the sequence you will need it. Develop a pattern of placement that is comfortable and efficient for you. Stick with it. Keep your work areas clean, uncluttered, and dry.

If you have practised loading the film and agitating the tank and have assembled all the materials you will need (see photograph), you are ready to begin. The photographs on this and the following five pages will guide you through processing a roll of film from start to finish. The steps shown include use of a stop-bath, hypo clearing agent, and a wetting agent, all of which are helpful and strongly recommended, but which can be eliminated if necessary.

●1. *Uncap film canister.* **One end of each canister is flat, the other end has a stub of spool. Uncap the flat end.**

●2. *Trim off film leader.* **The "leader" is the tapered end of a roll of film. The film will not feed onto the reel properly unless you remove the tapered section.**

●3. *Insert end of film in slot in centre of the reel.* **Remember to check that the reel spirals toward the film, and to squeeze the film to form a bow. Hold the film in the centre slot with your left index finger.**

●4. *Roll film onto reel.* **Keep the film straight, maintain a bow, and allow the film to slide between your right thumb and index finger. Run your left index finger along the film to check for kinks.**

Execute steps preceded by a "●" in complete darkness.

DEVELOPING BLACK-AND-WHITE FILM (continued) STEP-BY-STEP

● 5. *Cut spool away from end of film.* If you prefer, you can detach the spool by removing the tape that holds it to the film.

● 6. *Insert reel in developing tank.* If you are using a multi-reel tank but are developing only one reel of film, place the loaded reel in the bottom, and fill the remaining space with empty reels.

● 7. *Cover tank.* Once the tank's cover is on, you can turn on the lights.

● 8. *Pour measured amount of developer into a jug and check temperature.* Use enough developer to completely fill the tank, even if you have only one loaded reel in a multi-reel tank.

KODAK Packaged Developers	DEVELOPING TIMES IN MI					
	SMALL TANK†—Agitation at 30-Second Intervals					
	65°F 18°C	68°F 20°C	70°F 21°C	72°F 22°C	75°F 24°C	65°F 18°C
HC-110 (Dilution B)	8½	7½	6½	6	5	9½
D-76	9	8	7½	6½	5½	10
D-76 (1:1)	11	10	9½	9	8	13
MICRODOL-X	11	10	9½	9	8	13
MICRODOL-X (1:3)	–	–	15	14	13	–
POLYDOL	8	7	6½	6	5	9
DK-50 (1:1)	7	6	5½	5	4½	7½
HC-110 (Dilution A)	4¼	3¾	3¼	3	2½	4¾

NOTE: Do not use developers containing silver halide solvents.
*Unsatisfactory uniformity may result with development times shor
†Usually one-quart size or smaller.

● 9. *Determine correct development time.* Consult instructions packaged with your film or developer, or refer to a darkroom manual. A 23°C (73°F) temperature calls for a development time between 6½ minutes and 5½ minutes.

● 10. *Set timer.* The time indicated for this film in this developer at this temperature is 6 minutes. However, most people prefer to work at 20°C (68°F) which would require 8 minutes

50

11. *Pour developer in tank. Start timer.* Remember that pouring and timing being simultaneously. If you are using a tank holding three or more loaded reels, consider the alternative method for pouring developer described on p. 18.

12. *Agitate tank continuously for the first 30 seconds.* Thereafter, agitate for the last 5 seconds of each 30-second interval. Do not agitate in the final 30-second interval.

13. *Drain developer from tank.* Remember to begin pouring early enough so that the tank is empty when the timer rings (about 10 seconds for single-reel tanks). Discard the developer or save it for re-use, as applicable.

14. *Set timer.* The correct time for this particular stop bath is 30 seconds.

15. *Pour stop bath into tank. Start timer.* If you are not using a stop bath, insert a 30-second water wash here.

16. *Agitate tank.* Agitate continuously.

DEVELOPING BLACK-AND-WHITE FILM (continued)
STEP-BY-STEP

17. **Drain stop bath from tank.** Save the bath for re-use.

18. *Set timer.* The correct time for this particular fixer with this particular film is 4 minutes.

19. *Pour fixer in tank. Start timer.*

20. *Agitate tank.* Agitate continuously for the first 30 seconds. Thereafter, agitate for the last 5 seconds of each 30-second interval. Do not agitate in the final 30-second interval.

21. *Drain fixer from tank.* Save the fixer for re-use.

22. *Remove tank cover.*

23. *Wash film in running water.* A 1-minute wash is correct if a hypo clearing agent will be used. A water wash alone needs 20-30 minutes.

24. *Fill tank with hypo clearing agent. Agitate continuously.* Be certain you have diluted the clearing agent according to the manufacturer's instructions. The correct time to use with this particular brand of clearing agent is 1 minute.

25. *Wash in running water.* A 1-minute wash is sufficient.

26. *Prepare wetting agent.* Dilute according to the manufacturer's instructions.

27. *Pour wetting agent solution into tank.* Allow the film to soak for 30–60 seconds. Do not agitate. Discard the wetting agent or save it for re-use, as you wish.

28. *Hang film to dry. Squeegee.* Pre-moisten the squeegee tongs with a wetting agent solution. Run the tongs along the film in one continuous stroke from top to bottom. Try to protect the film from dust while drying.

CONTROLLING DENSITY AND CONTRAST

If density in a negative is incorrect, detail suffers. Only in the middle photograph is detail sufficient to yield a good print. In the top photograph, detail is obscured by excessive silver deposits, while in the bottom photograph, not enough silver has been deposited to provide adequate detail.

Dense Negative

Normally Dense Negative

Weak Negative

If the proper exposure of the *darkest* tone in a scene requires an aperture that is no more than seven stops different from the aperture required for a perfect exposure of the *lightest* tone (at the same shutter speed), the film will be able to record all the tones contained in the scene. (Of course, the actual photograph must be exposed for the tone exactly between the two extremes.) If a scene contains a tonal range greater than seven *f*-stops, that is, if the scene is too "contrasty" for the film, detail will be lost in the shadow and/or the highlight areas. If a scene contains a tonal range substantially less than seven *f*-stops, the film's capabilities are being under-utilized. Because of the nature of film developing, however, both these problems can be alleviated somewhat by manipulating negative density and contrast in the darkroom.

THE EFFECT OF DEVELOPMENT TIME

How development time affects density and contrast

When film is exposed to light, the conversion of silver halide to metallic silver is greatest where the largest amount of light hits the film; that is, the greatest amount of silver is deposited on the sections of the negative that correspond to the *highlights* in the original scene. Conversely, the least amount of silver is deposited on the areas of the negative that correspond to *shadows* in the original scene.

When exposed film comes in contact with developer, a large amount of silver halide must be converted to metallic silver in the highlight areas, but far less silver halide must be converted in the shadow areas. Thus, shadows finish developing relatively quickly, whereas highlights take much longer. If development is cut short before the highlights are completely developed, they appear more grey in a final print than they were in the original scene. In other words, *under-development reduces contrast* by reducing the range of tones (shades of grey) contained in the negative. If development is allowed to proceed *beyond* the time for an "optimal" negative, shadow density may increase a little, but highlight density increases substantially, causing an increase in overall contrast because the range of tones in the negative becomes wider. In other words, *over-development increases contrast*.

If a scene contains a tonal range which is greater than seven *f*-stops, under-developing the film will tend to reduce the tonal range (or contrast) on the negative so that the range falls within the film's recording capabilities. But since under-development will reduce the negative's overall density, the original scene needs to have been over-exposed to compensate. Therefore, if you are confronted with a high-contrast scene that exceeds your film's recording capability – an outdoor panorama under a harsh sun, for example – over-expose the scene by one *f*-stop, then under-develop the film. The

<table>
<tr><td colspan="2">DEVELOPMENT TIME AND
SUBJECT TONAL RANGE</td></tr>
</table>

**DEVELOPMENT TIME AND
SUBJECT TONAL RANGE**

If exposure meter readings reveal that a scene contains fewer or more than seven tones, you can "expand" or "contract" the scene's tonal range as suggested below.

If subject tonal range is:	Change development time by:
5 stops	+60%
6 stops	+25%
7 stops	no change
8 stops	2.5%
9 stops	−5%

→ 22   → 22A

result will be a negative of correct density which preserves the shadow and highlight detail that would have been lost had the scene been exposed and processed normally.

Likewise, if you wish to photograph a low-contrast scene – a sail-boat engulfed in fog, perhaps – under-exposing the film followed by over-developing the negative will produce a properly dense negative showing a broader tonal range (more contrast) than the original scene. Control such as this is what makes darkroom processing much more than a routine exercise in following instructions.

OTHER FACTORS

The amount of contrast displayed by a final print will not only be affected by the original scene, the way it is exposed, and the way it is developed, but also by the camera lens, the enlarger light source, and the enlarger lens.

Making adjustments to improve negatives

If the contrast in your negatives is consistently too high or too low, try decreasing or increasing development time, respectively, to alleviate the problem. If this causes a problem with density, set your exposure meter to a lower or higher ASA/ISO rating, respectively, which has the effect of altering exposure. (The rating assigned by the film's manufacturer applies under a "standard" set of conditions. Your equipment or conditions may invalidate the assigned ASA/ISO rating.)

Testing for proper negative contrast

A simple exercise will help you establish the best speed rating and development

time for your film-equipment-developer combination.

Load your camera with fresh film, and set your exposure meter to the film's assigned ASA/ISO setting. Next, photograph a grey scale available from photographic dealers, filling the film frame as completely as possible. Now reduce your ASA/ISO setting by one-half stop and repeat. Keep changing the setting by one-half stop until you have taken photographs at two consecutive settings on either side of the film's assigned ASA/ISO rating. Now, develop the film normally. The setting at which the individual squares on the grey scale are distinct is the setting you should normally use with this film. You can repeat the test for the other films you regularly use, and keep a record of the new ASA/ISO settings for future reference.

Being able to analyse contrast in a negative will help you learn to *control* **contrast and to decide on the grade of paper to use to print a particular negative.**

The negative at left, below, is too "contrasty". The difference between the lightest and darkest tones is extreme, and there is no detail in the darkest and lightest areas.

The negative at right, below, shows insufficient contrast. The gradations between tones are slight, and the frame appears dull overall.

The negative above demonstrates the way a negative *should* **look. The range of tones is not extreme, but the subject is nonetheless clearly defined. Note especially that detail is excellent in both the darkest and lightest areas.**

You will save yourself a substantial amount of printing paper as well as time if you quickly learn to identify and produce negatives showing correct density and contrast.

High Contrast Negative

Low Contrast Negative

PUSH PROCESSING

The use of available light is often desirable for artistic effect in subjects like this but the low level of light may require push-processing.

If you are faced with a situation in which there is insufficient light to allow you to take a picture at a fast enough shutter speed to prevent blurring, you may have to resort to "pushing" your film speed beyond its ASA/ISO rating. For example, suppose you are confronted by a situation such that even though you have set your lens to its widest aperture and are using ASA/ISO400 film, you are still worried that the shutter speed you need for a correct exposure might permit a blurred image. If you set your exposure meter to ASA/ISO 800, the meter will indicate that a correct exposure is occurring at the next faster shutter speed. The net effect is that the image on the film is "frozen" by the faster speed, and the film is under-exposed by one f-stop. Had you pushed the film to ASA/ISO1200, you could have used a shutter speed one-and-a-half times faster than at the 400 rating, and a push to 1600 would have allowed you to use a shutter speed two times faster than at ASA/ISO400.

Push-processing

Because pushed film contains under-exposed latent images, normal processing of such film produces negatives of less than optimal density. In order to improve density, you can either extend development time or use a special developer specifically intended for use in processing pushed film. (Of course, you must always push the *entire* roll of film, since you cannot push-process a few frames while processing the rest normally.)

Extending processing time

The more you have pushed a film (the more you have increased the film's notional speed above its recommended rating), the more you need to extend processing time if you are using a standard developer. Although the extended development time improves negative density, it also causes increased graininess, loss of sharpness, loss of detail in shadows and highlights, and

Temperature and Film Speed for Some High Speed Developers

Film	Temp F°	C°	Developer: Rated ASA/ISO–Development Time in Minutes*			
			Acuspeed	Microphen†	Unitol†	HC110
Tri-X	65°	18°	1200/7½	800/4	2400/8¼	1200/7
	70°	21°	1200/6	800/3½	2400/6¾	1200/5¼
	75°	24°	1200/4¾	800/3	2400/5½	1200/4
Plus-X	65°	18°	320/5	250/3½	400/3½	320/4
	70°	21°	320/4	250/3	400/2	320/3¼
	75°	24°	320/3¼	250/2½	400/2	320/2¾
HP-5	65°	18°	1600/10	800/4	1600/11	1000/6¼
	70°	21°	1600/8	800/3½	1600/8	1000/5¼
	75°	24°	1600/6¼	800/3	1600/5½	1000/4½
FP-4	65°	18°	200/5	250/4	320/3¾	320/4¼
	70°	21°	200/4	250/3½	320/3	320/3½
	75°	24°	200/3¼	250/3	320/2½	320/2¾

*NOTE: Pushing film involves some risk. Actual times may vary depending on circumstances and equipment. Experiment first, then make adjustments based on your findings. Dilutions are approximate and subject to testing.

†At recommended ratio of developer to water.

Push-processing

To push ASA/ISO 400 black and white film in Kodak D-76 or Ilford ID-11, try altering development time as shown in the chart below. The increases are only approximate, and you may need to adjust the suggested percentages according to your own results.

To push	To ASA/ISO	Increase development time by
2 stops	1600	80%
1½ stops	1200	60%
1 stop	800	40%

increased contrast. As you might expect, the more the film is pushed, the more noticeable these effects.

Using special developers
High-speed developers such as Acufine are formulated to minimize the image deterioration that occurs when pushed film is processed in standard developers. These special developers are excellent for preserving grain structure, shadow and highlight detail, sharpness, and contrast by controlling the clumping of metallic silver that otherwise occurs when film is pushed and push-processed.

Which to use
If you only occasionally resort to pushing film, there is little point in purchasing special developers. If you regularly push film, however, or if you have a roll of pushed film out of which you wish to squeeze every last drop of quality, then special developers are worthwhile.

Sometimes push-processing with high speed films can be done deliberately to create maximum grain for artistic effects which will be further enhanced by using a contrast printing paper.

REDUCTION AND INTENSIFICATION

Over-exposed Negative

REDUCING A NEGATIVE
The negative shown above was over-exposed by three *f*-stops and processed normally. Treatment with Farmer's Reducer reduced the over-exposed image to normal density, as shown below.

Often you can rectify minor density problems merely by choosing the correct grade of printing paper (as explained in the next chapter), but in extreme cases, two methods – *reduction* and *intensification* – exist for treating the negative itself before the print is made. These techniques, however, are best used only as a last resort.

REDUCING DENSITY

You can reduce negative density in two simple steps using Farmer's Reducer. Two solutions, A & B, are required. A is a 10% solution of potassium ferricyanide and B is a 20% hypo solution. This should not be acid hypo and must not contain hardener.

1. *Soak* the negative in water for 10 minutes.
2. *Mix* equal volumes of solutions A and B in a dish large enough to accommodate the negative you wish to treat.
3. *Immediately immerse* the negative in the mixture. The mixture has an active life of only 10 minutes.
4. *Watch* the negative closely; *do not over-reduce*. Over-reduced negatives are very difficult to restore.
5. *Remove* the negative as soon as reduction has progressed to your satisfaction.
6. *Wash* the negative in running water for at least 10 minutes.
7. *Dry* the negative.
8. *Repeat* the entire process, if necessary.

Reduced Negative

Under-exposed Negative

Intensified Negative

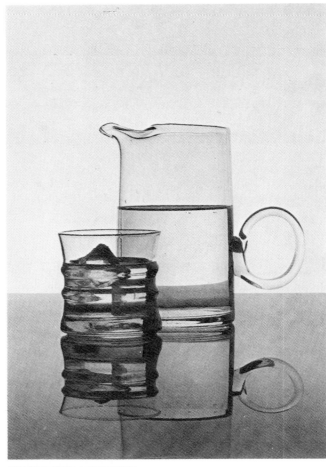

INTENSIFYING DENSITY

A negative that lacks density is referred to as being *weak*. Chromium Intensifier restores density and improves contrast but at the same time adds significantly to the grain size of the film.

Two solutions are required, A and B. A is made by dissolving 1 oz (28·3 g) of potassium bichromate in 20 oz (50 ml) of water and B consists of 2 oz (56 ml) of hydrochloric acid to 20 oz (560 ml) of water. For use A is diluted with six times its volume of water and an amount of B about four times the volume is added to it.

1. *Soak* the negative in water for about 10 minutes.
2. *Immerse* the negative in solution for 3–5 minutes, or until the entire image is bleached yellow.
3. *Rinse* in water until the negative clears and the yellow disappears.
4. *Re-develop* the negative in any fine grain developer until a darker image reappears.
5. *Wash* for 10–20 minutes.
6. *Repeat* the entire process, if necessary.

INTENSIFYING A NEGATIVE
When a negative has been under-exposed to the point where it is difficult to print (above, left), you may be able to salvage the negative by bleaching and re-developing it in a process known as *intensification*. Although intensification will yield a more printable negative (above, right), grain will increase and quality will remain inferior to that of a negative that was properly exposed and processed in the first place.

4. THE BLACK-AND-WHITE PRINT

When you expose a frame of film but allow someone else or a machine to develop and print it, for all practical purposes your involvement in the creative process has ended with the camera exposure. However, by processing and printing your own film, you assume a position of total control. You manipulate each facet of the craft until you achieve exactly the results *you* are seeking.

The mechanics of producing a high-quality print, while not very difficult to learn, require more than a simple reproduction of the image on a negative. With practice and determination, you can dramatically and creatively influence the appearance of a print – to an equal or even a greater extent than when you took the photograph originally. In other words, the negative is as much a starting point for creativity as the original scene. You will know you have achieved the highest level of darkroom mastery when you discover that the decisions you make regarding the way you take your photographs are influenced by the way you plan to process and print them.

The two phases of producing a print are: exposing the paper and processing it. The first phase is a "dry" procedure performed with the help of an enlarger, and the latter phase is a "wet" procedure in which chemicals in liquid form are required. Although you will need to combine the two phases once you actually start producing your own prints, we will discuss each phase separately.

The dry procedure, in which you expose the paper, is probably the most rewarding and exciting part of darkroom processing, perhaps because that is the phase in which you have the greatest creative influence. Although the selection of a printing paper can be an imposing task because of the bewildering array of paper available, the specific paper you initially choose is not critical as long as you come to know it well. Once you become thoroughly familiar with the way in which paper responds to exposure and processing, you will be able to switch to different papers with ease.

Unless you are planning to try archival printing, (see p. 78), the wet part of preparing prints varies little when using products from one manufacturer or another. Similarly, once you learn to process prints, the techniques are the same whether you are preparing a contact sheet, a test exposure, or a final print.

THE PRINTING SET-UP

A Leitz Focomat V35 enlarger for 35mm negatives has automatic focusing and built-in colour filters. There is an enormous range of enlargers in a very wide range of prices and this also applies to the masking frames.

PREPARING TO PRINT

Most of the equipment (dishes, tongs, thermometers, water, measures, etc.) that you need for black and white printing has already been described and discussed in the first two chapters. However, there are some other considerations you should have when you are making prints.

Chemicals

With some slight variations, the chemicals used to process prints are similar to those used to develop film. *Indicator stop baths* are normal stop baths with a chemical that changes colour and thereby indicates when the stop bath is exhausted and needs to be replaced. *Fixers* are usually the same in printing as in developing, although a special dilution may be necessary. Also, as with film, a *clearing agent* improves upon plain water washes.

Safelights

Since most papers are not panchromatic, and as a result do not respond to all colours of light, low-intensity red or amber colours often will not affect paper at all. Therefore, you can use safelights of these colours to allow you to see in the darkroom while the normal room lights are off. Because papers vary in sensitivity to safelight illumination, be sure to follow the manufacturer's instructions for the type of paper you are using. As a rule, you will be safe as long as your light source is of the proper colour, is produced by a bulb no stronger than 15 watts, and is located no closer than 4 ft (1.2 m) from the paper.

Cleanliness and care

Any speck of dust on the negative will block light and produce a white spot on the final print. Although you can "spot" or retouch prints, you will save yourself later effort by making certain your negative is scrupulously clean when you use it

to expose the print. An anti-static brush and a can of compressed air will remove dust easily and effectively. If your negative has become scratched or nicked, glycerine or a proprietary solution applied according to the manufacturer's instructions will help. A magnifying glass such as the Agfa 8x lupe will assist you to inspect negatives for dust and scratches.

Tongs

Although some photographers use their hands to transfer prints from dish to dish, that technique invites contamination of the print caused by chemicals clinging to the fingertips. The safe way to transfer paper from dish to dish is to use tongs – a separate pair for each dish.

Temperature

More important than keeping a specific temperature for each chemical is keeping all chemicals at the *same* temperature during processing. Room temperature of around 20°C (68°F) is adequate, but make certain that any water you draw from the tap is adjusted to the same temperature as your other chemicals.

WET-SIDE SUPPLIES

1. **Wash dish and siphon**
2. **Timer**
3. **Paper towels**
4. **Processing dishes and tongs**
5. **Developer**
6. **Stop bath**
7. **Fixer**
8. **22 oz or 44 oz (600 or 1200 ml) graduated jug and thermometer**
9. **Print-drying squeegee**
10. **Print dryer**

PRINTING PAPER

Not all negatives are best printed on normal grade 2 paper. In the top photograph, harsh midday sunlight produced such deep shadows and bright highlights that the range of light intensities in the scene exceeded the film's ability to record them. Moreover, what little detail *was* present in the shadows and highlights of the negative did not show up on grade 2 paper. Printing the same negative on grade 1 paper would have caused more shadow and highlight detail to appear.

In the middle photograph, the range of contrasts on the negative was so uniform that the image appeared dull when printed on grade 2 paper. Had this negative been printed on grade 3 paper, contrast would have been improved and the print made more interesting.

The bottom picture shows a subject which is almost beyond the range of the paper and the shadow portion needed shading during enlarging in order to retain detail.

TYPES OF PAPER

If you have never made your own prints, you might initially feel overwhelmed by the wide assortment of black and white papers on the market. However, you can quickly become quite knowledgeable by asking your photographic dealer to show you a sample of books of papers by Ilford, Kentmere or Kodak. If you have never seen any paper other than that used by commercial processing laboratories, you may be surprised at the variety of surface textures, colours and weights available. Study and compare the samples carefully to gain a feel for the way papers differ.

Described below are some terms you will find printed on the labels of the boxes in which papers are sold. By being familiar with their definitions before you enter the shop, you will be able to decide quickly upon the type of paper you want to buy.

Base

Historically, photographic emulsions were mounted on fibre-base papers. Recently, however, resin-coated papers such as Kodak RC and Ilford Ilfospeed have been introduced which are water resistant. This type of paper requires a much shorter processing time and dries more quickly than its untreated counterparts. Because water-resistant paper is a new development, no one knows for certain how quickly it will deteriorate over years or decades. Nevertheless, there is no question that water-resistant papers are a convenience.

Weight

Papers are sold in two thicknesses – light (or single) weight and heavy (or double) weight. Lightweight papers are satisfactory for prints up to 8″ x 10″ (20 x 25 cm), but are too fragile for larger size prints.

Surface

Paper surfaces differ in terms of texture and luminosity. *Texture* refers to the degree of smoothness shown by a paper's surface. Common textures include glossy, lustre, semi-matt, and matt. *Luminosity* is closely related to texture and refers to the brilliance shown by the paper's surface. Glossy and lustre surfaces show high luminosity, whereas matt surfaces are noticeably duller.

If you would like to, you can further enhance the shine of glossy paper by means of *ferrotyping*, a process in which you dry the paper face down on a highly polished sheet of chromium plated tin. However, you may well find that the high glare produced by ferrotyping is a distraction.

As a rule, you want a glossy surface if your print will be reproduced (for example, in a newspaper or magazine). If you plan to display the print itself, selecting a more textured surface will help to minimize surface glare. Keep in mind, however, that image sharpness decreases as surface texture increases.

CONTRAST GRADES

Contrast

Every negative contains a certain number of tones (shades of grey) between total black and total white. Likewise, each photographic paper *produces* a certain number of tones between black and white. When the tonal sensitivity of the paper corresponds to the number of distinct tones present in the negative, you obtain a print as "true" to the negative as you can achieve.

The number and range of distinct tones that a paper can produce is indicated by its *contrast grade number*. The tonal range of grade 2 papers, usually described as "normal", roughly corresponds to the full range of tones that black and white film can record. Printing a negative containing this range of tones on a higher grade of paper would reduce the number of tones contained in the final print. Because this would result in fewer gradations between the remaining tones, the print would display increased contrast. On the other hand, printing the negative on a *lower* grade of paper would preserve all the tones in the negative but would reduce the separation between the individual tones. As a result, the contrast would be decreased.

In short, different paper grades provide you with a means for controlling or correcting the contrast of your final prints. For example, suppose you have photographed a scene under harsh sunlight such that your negative displays a high degree of contrast. If you print on grade 1 paper, the printed image will show a more normal range of tones than is on the negative. Likewise, if you have shot a scene on a hazy day, and have produced a low-contrast negative, you can print on high-contrast paper to generate a more normal range of tones.

Variable grade papers

The wider the variation in amount of contrast from one negative to the next, the greater the number of paper grades you will need – unless you use a variable grade paper such as Ilford Multigrade. With these papers, you can change contrast grade by placing special filters in front of your enlarger lens. (Actually, the filters can be assembled from colour printing filters, so if you have a dichroic head, you can control the paper's contrast by "dialling in" the correct filtration. Consult your owner's manuals for details.)

Traditional papers are sold in contrast grades of 1, 2, 3, 4, and 5, whereas variable grade papers can produce contrast grades of 1, $1\frac{1}{2}$, 2, $2\frac{1}{2}$, 3, $3\frac{1}{2}$, and 4. As you can see, variable grade papers can produce intermediate-value contrasts for "fine tuning", but cannot reach the extreme contrast grades possible with single grade papers. Also, bear in mind that the grade designations are not always interchangeable; that is, for any individual paper grade, the Multigrade equivalent may produce slightly higher or lower contrast.

Paper tone

The term *black* actually encompasses several different colour tones. *True black* refers to a neutral black tone, while black with a cream tone is said to be *warm*, and black with a blue tone is said to be *cold*.

In the early years of photographic printing, the choice of paper was considered an important aesthetic judgement, and photographers sometimes rendered their blacks in shades of green, blue, orange, and other colours. Today, the range of paper tones available is very limited, and most photographers do not even consider any tone other than neutral black – even though a change of paper tone can aesthetically improve the final print.

You can influence the tone characteristic of an image through your choice of paper or by employing one of the colour toners available from photographic dealers.

PROCESSING THE PRINT
Step by step

WET SIDE ARRANGEMENT
Even before you expose a sheet of printing paper, you should prepare the supplies and equipment you will need in order to process it. Mix the necessary chemicals, pour them into dishes, arrange the dishes in the order that you will use them, and provide for a water wash.

A print is processed for any of three purposes: to produce a contact print, to make an exposure test, or to produce a final print. In each case, you should process the paper as soon as it is exposed. Since the general procedure for processing prints is the same for contact printing, determining exposure, and final printing, we will discuss it first, before discussing the specific procedures for each case.

PRELIMINARIES

Print processing is very closely related to film processing, but it has the advantage of allowing you to see what you are doing under a safelight of the correct colour. Before you begin to process a print, be certain you have prepared the chemicals shown in the photograph above and have assembled all the equipment you will need. The time shown in the instructions at right for developing the print is 1½ minutes. This is the recommended time for fibrebase papers, but if you are developing a resin-coated paper, the recommended time is only 1 minute. Under-developing a print causes its blacks to appear grey; over-developing has little effect up to 3 minutes of total processing time and no effect at all after that. As a general rule, you should process fibrebase papers for no less than 1 minute and no more than 3 minutes, whereas you should process resin-coated papers for no less than 45 seconds and no more than 2 minutes.

1. *Immerse exposed paper in developer. Start timer.* Immerse the print by sliding it in as shown to ensure that liquid covers the entire surface all at once. The timer should be set to 1½ minutes for fibre-base papers, 1 minute for resin-coated papers.

2. *Agitate.* As the image starts to appear, gently rock the dish back and forth to establish a wave motion in the liquid.

3. *Remove paper. Drain.*

. . . and allow the liquid on the surface of the paper to drain into the dish for a few seconds before continuing to the next step.

4. *Immerse print in stop bath. Start timer.*

5. *Agitate in stop bath* for 10 seconds.

PROCESSING THE PRINT (Continued)
Step by step

6. *Remove print. Drain.*

7. *Immerse print in fixer.* The print should be left in the fixer between 2 minutes and 10 minutes, depending on the paper and the type of fixer. The heavier the paper and the more exhausted the fixer, the longer the time should be. Consult the instructions packaged with the fixer.

8. *Agitate.* Continue to agitate the dish as long as the print is in the fixer.

9. *Remove print. Immerse print in water wash.* Wash fibre-base papers for 60 minutes, resin-coated papers for 4 minutes.

10. *Squeegee print.* First run the squeegee across the back of the print, then across the front.

11. *Dry print.* Either use a drying rack or place the print on absorbent paper.

The sudden appearance of the image on your
very first print, which you have exposed and
processed entirely on your own, is one of the
most exciting experiences in photography.

CONTACT PRINTING

1. *Adjust enlarger head* so that the lamp produces a patch of light on the baseboard slightly larger than the paper you are using.
2. *Turn off all lights except safelight.*

3. *Insert sheet of printing paper,* emulsion side *up,* into your contact printing frame.
4. *Arrange strips of negatives* along the length of the paper, emulsion side *down.* (Six strips will just squeeze onto an 8" x 10" (20 x 25 cm) sheet of paper.)

5. *Lay glass cover on top negatives.*
6. *Set enlarger lens to f/8.* or thereabout.

7. *Turn on enlarger lamp* for 3–8 seconds. (See the section on determining exposure, page 72).
8. *Develop print normally.*

THE ROLL AT A GLANCE

Once you have developed a roll of film, you must decide which frames you want to print. Although with practice you can learn to "read" negatives fairly well, usually you will want to make printing decisions based upon a *contact print* of the entire roll of film.

To make a contact print, you place the entire roll of film in direct contact with a single sheet of printing paper, turn on your enlarger long enough to properly expose the paper, and then process the paper in the normal manner. The resulting print will contain a positive image of each frame on the roll.

Actually, contact printing and determining exposure are inter-related: you cannot make a contact print without some idea of the best exposure time, but you usually do not want to make a test exposure before you have made a contact print. Therefore, familiarize yourself with both these topics before attempting either.

Contact printing frames

In order to hold the film flat against the paper, you will need to use a contact printing frame. You can either purchase a frame or make one of your own. All you need is a wooden frame that will hold a sheet of printing paper, and a sheet of glass to lay over the film to hold it flat. Hinge one edge of the glass to the frame with tape.

Paper

In most circumstances, normal grade 2 paper will produce satisfactory contact prints. However, you may find that the increased contrast of grade 3 paper will make your contacts easier to read.

A 36-frame roll of film cut into six strips of six frames each will just fit onto a standard 8" x 10" sheet of printing paper.

Making a contact

To make a contact print, first cut your roll of 35mm film into strips of six frames each, then follow the instructions at right.

DETERMINING EXPOSURE

A printing aid, such as Kodak's Enlarging Negative, makes it easy to establish exposure time. Place your negative in the enlarger, focus, and set the lens to *f*/8. Then put the scale on top of your test paper and make a 60-second exposure. After the print is developed, you can select the best exposure time by examining the print and identifying the band that looks best.

EVALUATING A TEST PRINT

Each strip in your test print corresponds to a different exposure time. The lightest strip represents the shortest exposure, the darkest strip the longest. The strip that shows the best exposure indicates the amount of time to expose the final print. For example, in the above photograph, the third strip from the right was given the best exposure time. Since each strip in this example represents an additional five seconds of exposure, the correct exposure for the final print is fifteen seconds.

If all the strips are too dark, you need to repeat the test using a smaller lens aperture and/or a shorter exposure time. If all strips are too light, repeat the test using a larger lens aperture and/or a longer exposure time.

If your test print indicates that an inconveniently long exposure time is needed, you can cut the time by one-half by opening the lens one *f*-stop, or by one-quarter by opening the lens two *f*-stops, and so on. Likewise, you can increase a very short exposure time by closing down the lens and increasing the time to correspond.

APERTURE AND EXPOSURE TIME

If all negatives were of equal density, and if you always enlarged prints to the same degree, you would always use the same exposure time and lens opening. However, since conditions do vary, you need to make a test print that includes different exposures from which you can select the best. An excellent technique is to expose different sections of a single print for different lengths of time. After the paper is processed, the section that looks best indicates the setting at which you should make the final exposure.

Exposure

The relationship between lens aperture, exposure time, and printing paper is analogous to the relationship between lens aperture, shutter speed, and film in a camera. In the darkroom, a proper exposure depends on using the correct combination of aperture and exposure time for the amount of light being generated and the sensitivity of the paper. Closing or opening the enlarger lens one *f*-stop has the same effect on degree of exposure as halving or doubling the exposure time; that is, *f*-stop and exposure time are reciprocal. For example, *f*/8 at 3 seconds is equivalent to *f*/11 at 6 seconds, *f*/16 at 12 seconds, and so on.

Making a test print

The procedure for making a test print is similar to that for making a final print, which is illustrated on pp. 74–75. Before making a test print for the first time, read those pages so that you understand how making the test exposure fits into the overall process. Then make the test print by following the step by step description at right. Evaluate your results as described in the photograph above.

DETERMINING EXPOSURE

1. *Adjust enlarger height. Focus image.* The test image must be enlarged to the same size as you want the final print to be.

2. *Set lens to f/8 or f/11. Turn off enlarger lamp.* The specific setting is arbitrary, but f/8 and f/11 are intermediate apertures that provide good depth of field yet allow flexibility should your test reveal that a major exposure adjustment is necessary.

3. *Set timer. Place paper in the frame.* The greater the degree of enlargement, the longer the time duration should be. For small prints (smaller than 8″ x 10″) (20 x 25 cm), try 3, 4, or 5 seconds. For larger prints (12″ x 15″ or larger) (30x40 cm) try 10, 12, or 14 seconds.

4. *Cover all except last sixth of paper. Expose print.* Cover the print with a sheet of dark cardboard. Hold the cardboard motionless while the enlarger lamp is on.

5. *Uncover one additional sixth of paper. Expose again.* Continue repeating this step until the entire sheet of paper has been exposed, one additional strip at a time. (Note: You can expose the test print in quarters, fifths, sevenths, or other fractions, if you prefer.)

6. *Process print normally. Evaluate results.* Processing is described beginning on p. 67. How to evaluate the test print is explained on the page opposite.

EXPOSING THE PRINT
Step by step

EXPOSING THE PRINT

Once you have developed a roll of film, made a contact print, decided on an individual frame to enlarge, selected a paper to print on, and made a test exposure, you are ready to expose the final print following the procedures below.

EXPOSING THE PRINT

1. *Identify emulsion side of negative.* Dry film is bowed so that the emulsion lies on the *inside* of the bow.

2. *Clean negative.* Usually a blast from an air blower is sufficient to remove all dust, but sometimes you may also need to use an anti-static brush or even a liquid film cleaner.

3. *Insert negative into enlarger,* emulsion side down. Be certain the negative is properly aligned in the negative carrier and is held firmly.

4. *Adjust enlarger height. Focus image.* You can focus easily and accurately if you open your lens to its widest aperture.

5. *Select f-stop setting.* Use the same aperture you used to make your test print.

6. *Set timer.* Use the time that your test print indicated would give the best exposure.

7. *Turn off enlarger lamp. Remove sheet of printing paper from storage.* Be sure that the only illumination is from a safelight of the correct colour for the paper you are using.

8. *Identify emulsion side of paper.* The emulsion side is usually the shinier side.

9. *Place paper in easel*, emulsion side up.

10. *Expose print.* The procedures for processing the print after exposure are explained on p. 66.

DODGING AND BURNING-IN

TOOLS FOR DODGING AND AND BURNING-IN

Tools for dodging and burning-in are quite simple to make. Pieces of dark paper or cardboard with holes of various sizes and shapes will help to burn-in small areas.

You can make a wide variety of dodging tools by cutting circles, squares, and other shapes from cardboard and gluing them to a coat-hanger wire. The piece of Cellophane attached to one end of the wire in the above photograph softens the image (makes it somewhat less distinct) while allowing light to pass through to darken the dodged area.

DODGING

Selectively holding back some of the light from one part of the print (in this case the woman's face) is easy if you use one of the tools shown in the photograph at the top of this page. Keep the wand in constant motion and don't let the handle remain over any one area during the exposure; otherwise, a distinct circular edge will form around the dodged area, and a line will appear where the shadow of the handle falls on the paper.

BURNING-IN

By placing a piece of paper with a hole in its centre in the path of the light projected by your enlarger, you can selectively allow more light to reach one area of a print than another. In the photograph above the entire print was exposed for 20 seconds, then the face was given an additional 5-second exposure. Keep your burning-in tool in constant motion to prevent a distinct outline of the hole from appearing around the burned-in area.

TOTAL EXPOSURE CONTROL

The primary difference between film and printing paper is the base on which the light-sensitive emulsions are applied: film has a transparent base, printing paper has an opaque base. Not surprisingly, the same variations that occur in the developing rate of shadows and highlights on film occur on paper as well. With film, you can affect the appearance of shadows and highlights by altering the development time, but you cannot selectively affect one area more than another. With paper, because of the comparatively long exposure times and the fact that you can see the image during exposure, you can locally manipulate the appearance of shadows and highlights.

Suppose you make a print in which shadow detail has been lost. If you shorten the printing time to bring out the shadow detail, you will lose highlight detail and the print will appear too light overall. However, if you could selectively reduce the shadow exposure time, while exposing the rest of the print normally, your print would have both shadow detail and a correct overall exposure. The technique for holding back shadow exposure is called *dodging*.

Similarly, if your properly exposed print has insufficient highlight detail, your goal is to expose the overall print normally but to allow extra exposure time in the highlight areas. The technique to use in this case is called *burning-in*.

Dodging

Dodging involves blocking a portion of an image for part of the exposure time in order to make that portion lighter. For example, if a print's overall exposure requirement is 20 seconds, but you have found from your exposure test that 15 seconds is better for the shadow area, then for 5 seconds during the exposure you should block light by placing an opaque object in the light path between the enlarger lens and that area of the print. The devices you use for dodging can be a piece of cardboard or your hand for large areas, and specially constructed dodgers, such as the ones illustrated here, for small areas.

The technique of dodging is not difficult to learn. The only general rule is that you should constantly move the dodging instrument with a circular motion to prevent a sharp edge from occurring around the dodged area.

Burning-in

Burning-in involves blocking light for part of the exposure time from all areas except the area you want to darken in the print. For example, if the overall exposure requirement is 20 seconds, but you have found from your exposure test that 30 seconds is better for the highlights, then set your timer for a 30-second exposure. After 20 seconds, place something in the light path to block all light except that hitting the highlight area.

Instruments for burning-in can be a piece of cardboard with a hole in it or your hands held in such a way that most light is blocked. As with dodging, you should take care to keep your mask moving in small circles to prevent a sharp outline from forming.

With experience you will learn to combine both dodging and burning-in on the same print, thereby greatly extending your printing capabilities.

Straight Print

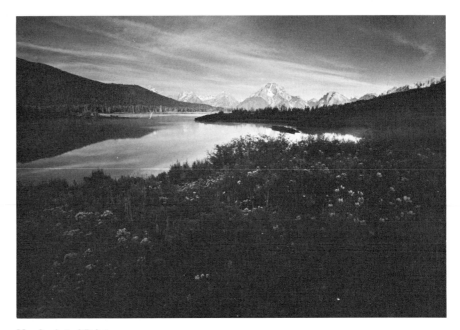

Manipulated Print

COMBINING DODGING AND BURNING-IN

Confronted by the scene above and relying only on your eye, you might think that the hills and flowers were recorded on film with equal density. However, the top photograph, which is a straight print from the negative, shows that the early morning sun spilling across the distant mountains had not been high enough to light up the foreground. When printing the bottom photograph, some light was blocked from the flower section by dodging during the exposure. The sky was then given extra exposure by burning-in. In both cases, the tool used was the photographer's hand.

Note also how burning-in the mountain on the left made it darker and thereby improved the composition by leading the viewer's eye toward the main subject, the distant mountains.

PRINTING FOR PERMANENCE

AN ARCHIVAL PROCESSING KIT
Ilford manufactures the Ilfobrom Archival Processing Kit which contains chemistry specifically designed for archival printing. Although archival printing is not difficult to perform for anyone familiar with black and white processing, the kit does offer the convenience of having all the necessary chemicals packaged together along with detailed instructions for their use. (Note that Ilford's archival-processing procedure differs from the general procedure described here.)

ARCHIVAL PROCESSING

Unless a conventionally processed black and white print is exposed to extreme conditions, it can survive for decades without special attention. Many photographs have lasted fifty years or more without becoming faded or discoloured. Nonetheless, if you wish to guarantee that a photograph retains its appearance as long as possible, or if you expect a photograph to encounter harsh conditions, *archival processing* will enhance its likelihood of enjoying a long life. Since a print's destruction can be caused by the very chemicals used to create the image in the first place, archival processing removes the last traces of these chemicals and then adds a protective coating of selenium or gold to further preserve the image.

Paper

Because fibre-base papers are absorbent, they retain some of the chemicals used to process the image. Even an overnight wash will not remove all vestiges of the chemicals. (Since resin-coated papers absorb very little moisture, they do not benefit from the traditional techniques of archival processing.)

Double fixing

As already discussed, the fixing step in film and print processing removes un-exposed silver halide compounds from the film or paper's emulsion layer. Therefore, the first stage in archival processing is to immerse the print in the fixer a second time to be absolutely certain that the fixing process has reached completion. The procedure is to prepare two solutions of fixer and immerse the print into each for five minutes. Most of the fixing activity occurs in the first solution, and the second finishes the process. Discard the fixer in the first dish when it becomes exhausted, and replace it with the second solution, which is still at nearly full strength. Then prepare fresh fixer and pour it into what becomes the new second solution.

Removing residual fixer

When you remove the print from the second fixer, residues of fixer as well as compounds of fixer and silver still cling to the paper. To remove residues, treat the print with a solution of Hypo Clearing Agent followed by a thorough wash in water. Finally, remove the last traces of fixer by immersing the print in a hypo eliminator.

Coating the image

By depositing a thin layer of selenium or gold over the image, you protect it from pollutants in the air. You can add selenium toner directly to the hypo clearing agent (2 oz (56 ml) of toner per gallon of hypo clearing agent), but you can add gold toner only after the hypo eliminator has been removed by a thorough wash in water.

HYPO ELIMINATOR
1. Add $\frac{1}{2}$ oz (14 ml) of concentrated (28%) ammonia to 5 oz (142 ml) of water.
2. Mix together $3\frac{1}{2}$ oz (100 ml) of the ammonia solution, $4\frac{1}{2}$ oz (128 ml) of 3% hydrogen peroxide solution, and 7 oz (490 ml) of water.
3. Add additional water to bring total volume to 32 oz (1 litre).
Caution: Store the hypo clearing solution in an *open* bottle to prevent the gases formed from breaking the bottle.

ARCHIVAL PRINTING, STEP BY STEP

1. *Prepare two dishes of fixer, one of hypo clearing agent, and one of hypo eliminator.*
2. *Develop print as usual.*
3. *Immerse print in stop bath as usual.*
4. *Immerse print in first fixer for 3–5 minutes (depending on paper weight).*
5. *Transfer print to second fixer for an additional 3–5 minutes.*
6. *Wash in water for 30–60 seconds.*
7. *Immerse print in hypo clearing agent for 2–3 minutes.*
8. *Wash in water for 10–20 minutes.*
9. *Immerse print in hypo eliminator for 6 minutes (with selenium toner added, if applicable).*
10. *Wash in water for 10 minutes.*
11. *Immerse in gold toner, if applicable.*
12. *Wash in water for 10 minutes.*

Thorough washing is vital for archival permanence. The photo below shows a simple but effective washer which draws off the hypo at the bottom of the slope. The photograph underneath shows a reciprocating washer that takes twelve prints at once, and it also draws the hypo from the base where it tends to remain in washers which do not have this facility.

ARCHIVAL PROCESSING

Procedure	Time	Comment
Develop normally		
Acid stop bath	30 sec.	
First fixing bath	3–5 min.	
Second fixing bath	3–5 min.	
Water rinse	30–60 sec.	
Hypo cleaning agent	2–3 min.	Agitate constantly
Hypo eliminator	6 min.	
Water	10 min.	
Gold toner*	10 min.	Use immediately after mixing
Water	10 min.	
Dry normally		Use acid-free blotter

*Selenium or other less expensive toners can be substituted.

CREATIVE TONING

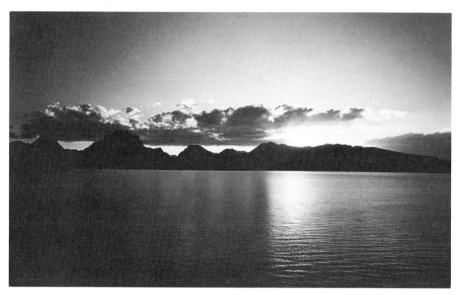

You can introduce a variety of different colours into a print by using one or more of the many toners available from photographic dealers.

The bottles shown in the photograph contain colour toners made by Edwal. Inside each bottle cap is a small container in which crystals are stored until it is time to use the toner. Once the crystals and the liquid have been mixed, the toning solution has a shelf life of three to four weeks. The number of 8″ x 10″ prints a bottle can tone depends upon the length of time the prints are allowed to remain in the toner.

The packets shown in the photograph above contain the powders which, when mixed with water, become the bleach and toning solutions used to sepia tone a print. Once mixed, the solutions have an indefinite shelf life. One set of packets is sufficient for toning forty 8″ x 10″ prints.

The photographs shown on the next page illustrate the results of applying Kodak sepia toner and Edwal colour toners to the black and white print reproduced above.

CREATIVE TONING

Beyond the capacity to protect a print from the ravages of time, toning can be used creatively to alter the colour in a black and white photograph. Toners work by replacing the blacks (oxidized silver) in a print. Although some toning processes are complex and difficult to perform, most toners are easy to mix, easy to store and easy to use. In addition, toning takes place at room temperature and under normal room lighting.

The toners most commonly used are shades of the colour brown. Sepia toners especially are very popular, but products which generate almost any colour are readily available from photographic dealers.

The toning instructions provided by manufacturers are clear and easy to follow, but read all warnings carefully to avoid accidentally producing dangerous fumes. Below are summaries of the important steps involved in two of the many toning procedures available.

KODAK SEPIA TONER

Kodak sepia toning involves two basic stages, plus an optional step.

In the first stage you immerse the print in a bleach solution which you have previously prepared. Within one minute (slightly longer for very dark prints) the image will have disappeared or turned a very pale yellow, at which time you remove the print and wash it in water for two minutes.

In the second stage you immerse the print in a toning solution, also previously prepared, for thirty seconds or as long as necessary for the toning process to run to completion.

Finally, because the toning process softens the print's emulsion layer, you have the option of immersing the print in a hardening bath (available from photographic dealers) to protect the print from damage.

EDWAL COLOUR TONERS

In addition to the colour brown, the Edwal colour toners offer you the opportunity to add the colours blue, red, green and yellow to a print. Because Edwal toners do not involve a bleaching step, they are even easier to use than Kodak's Sepia Toner.

To use an Edwal toner, you mix and dilute the toner crystals in accordance with the manufacturer's instructions. Next, you immerse a thoroughly washed, still wet print in the toning solution. By monitoring the progress of the toning reaction, you can decide when to remove the print. The longer you allow the print to remain in the toner, the more brilliant the final colour will be. Since you can add additional toner but you cannot remove toner once it has replaced the silver in a print, you should remove and wash the print for one minute while you are still certain that you have not toned the print more than you want, then immerse it again in toner, if necessary. A final wash of five minutes halts the toning process completely.

Usually, the print will look better with the white border trimmed off.

In a sepia-toned print the rich brown colour illustrated here replaces the black tones originally present. Unlike the Edwal colours shown below, sepia toning is an all or nothing process in that all of the black present in the original print is completely replaced by the colour brown.

All three of these photographs were toned with Edwal colour toners. Red toner was used in the photograph at bottom left and blue toner at bottom right.

The multi-colour effect present in the upper photograph is possible because the Edwal toning process need not run to completion. In this instance, the print was immersed for only two minutes in blue toner, washed, and then immersed in red toner for another three minutes. The second immersion caused the remaining silver oxide granules to be replaced by the red tone.

You can limit toning to selected portions of a print either by applying the toner carefully with a small paint brush or by masking areas with rubber cement before immersing the print in the toner. After the print is toned, the cement can be easily removed by rubbing. Interesting effects are possible by toning one section of a print one colour and another section a different colour.

Edwal toners are not easily obtainable in the United Kingdom but similar toners are available in the Tetenal range imported by Johnsons of Hendon Limited.

5. PROCESSING COLOUR FILM

You do not need fully to understand the underlying principles of colour photography in order to perform the mechanical operations involved in developing and printing colour film. However, if you know the whys of colour processing as well as the hows, you will be able to master the procedures much more efficiently.

Modern colour photography exploits the phenomenon that any colour in the visible spectrum can be produced by some combination of the *primary* colours, blue, green, and red. Colour film and colour processing use those three colours to reproduce the entire range of colours encountered in nature.

The specific method usually used is called the *subtractive* method and involves passing white light (which contains all colours) through filters which block selected colours but allow other colours to pass. The effect of the filters is to subtract from the white light all colours except one. That one colour then continues through the filters unhindered.

Three filters are involved in the subtractive method: a yellow filter (which blocks blue light but passes green and red light), a magenta filter (which blocks green light and passes blue and red), and a cyan filter (which blocks red light and passes blue and green.

Thus, with the proper combination of yellow, magenta and cyan filters, each of the three primary colours (blue, green, red) can be produced subtractively from white light.

HOW THE COLOUR PROCESS WORKS

HOW A COLOUR TRANSPARENCY IS MADE

1. The image in this example, a red cloth, forms a black and white image on the red-sensitive layer of a frame of colour film, but leaves the blue- and green-sensitive layers unaffected.

2. During processing the images are reversed: the image on the red layer is transferred to both the blue and green layers. The blue layer is dyed yellow, and the green layer is dyed magenta, but the red layer is *not* dyed cyan.

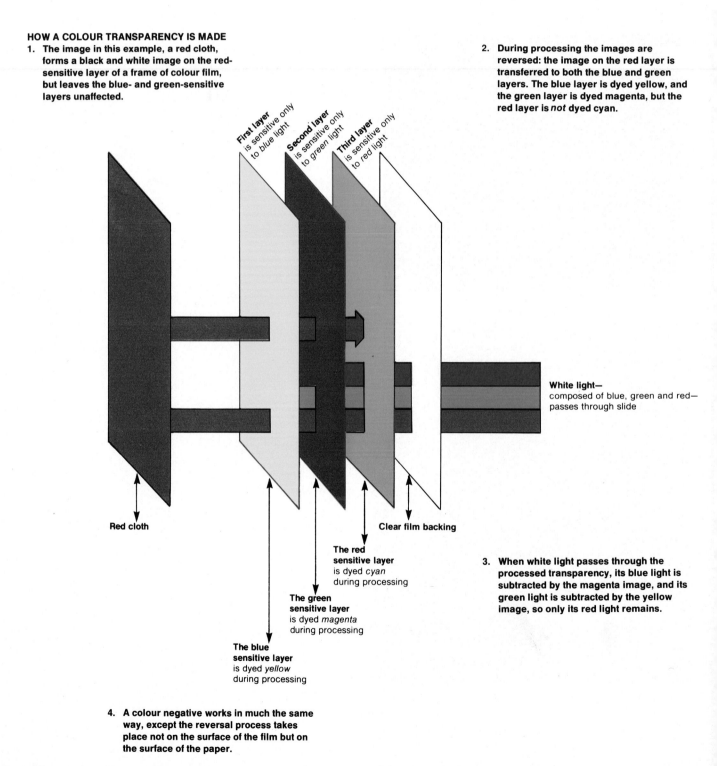

First layer is sensitive only to *blue* light

Second layer is sensitive only to *green* light

Third layer is sensitive only to *red* light

White light— composed of blue, green and red— passes through slide

Red cloth

Clear film backing

The red sensitive layer is dyed *cyan* during processing

The green sensitive layer is dyed *magenta* during processing

The blue sensitive layer is dyed *yellow* during processing

3. When white light passes through the processed transparency, its blue light is subtracted by the magenta image, and its green light is subtracted by the yellow image, so only its red light remains.

4. A colour negative works in much the same way, except the reversal process takes place not on the surface of the film but on the surface of the paper.

COLOUR TEST CHART

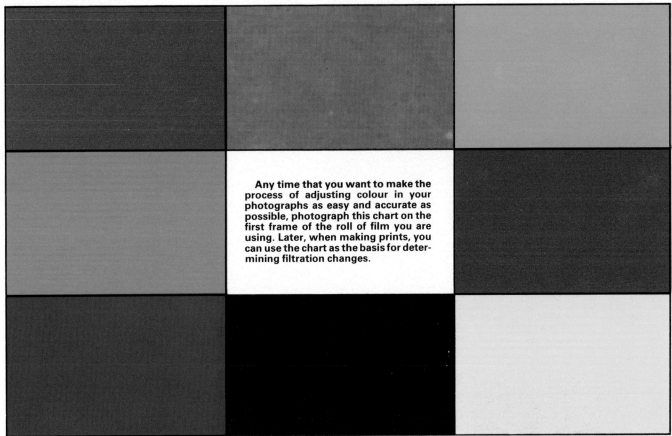

Any time that you want to make the process of adjusting colour in your photographs as easy and accurate as possible, photograph this chart on the first frame of the roll of film you are using. Later, when making prints, you can use the chart as the basis for determining filtration changes.

Colour film is coated with three separate layers of *emulsion*, one layer responsive to blue light, one layer responsive to green light, and one layer responsive to red light. Light striking a segment of colour film causes changes in whichever emulsion layers are sensitive to the colours contained in the light, and in a sense, the emulsion layers capture the light. Later, processing of the film creates subtractive filter layers capable of reproducing the original colour.

For example let us assume that a photograph is being taken of a piece of red cloth and that its image fills the entire frame of film. The red-sensitive emulsion layer on the film would respond, but the other two layers would not respond.

Since red is generated by passing white light through the combination of a magenta filter and a yellow filter, pro-cessing the frame of film in this example will ultimately produce one magenta filter layer and one yellow filter layer. Once these filter layers are produced, white light projected through them (either from a projector bulb or from the light reflected off the white backing of printing paper) will be reduced to red light, thereby reproducing the original colour. Let us see how processing accomplishes this task.

When a light-sensitive emulsion layer responds to a colour, a *black and white* latent, or underdeveloped, image – not a colour image – is formed in that layer. Colour in the form of dyes is coupled to the black and white image later, during the course of processing. Therefore, when red light strikes the film in our example, a black and white latent image is formed in the film's red-sensitive layer.

Dye *couplers* must then be added before a colour image is formed.

The specific steps involved in converting the black and white image into a colour image differ depending on whether the final product is to be a transparency or a print. In the case of transparencies, the processed film itself is viewed. Therefore, the colour of the original scene must be generated in the film. In the case of prints, the film is not viewed; instead, it is used to reproduce the colours of the original scene on a *sheet of printing paper*. Therefore, the colours present on print film after processing are not the final colours on the print, or the colours that were present in the original scene.

The illustration on this page summarizes how colour is produced in transparencies and negatives.

HOW THE COLOUR PROCESS WORKS
(Continued)

EMULSION LAYER RESPONSES

Each point on the three emulsion layers of colour film responds proportionately to the amount of blue, green, and red present in a scene. If the light striking a point is of a primary colour (that is, if its colour is pure blue, pure green, or pure red), only one emulsion layer will respond. If the light striking a point is not of a primary colour, then its colour is a *mixture* of primary colours, and more than one emulsion layer will respond. Furthermore, the relative densities of the images formed on the layers will be proportional to the relative contribution of each primary colour to the mixed colour. For example, the colour purple will form an image on both the blue and red emulsion layers, but the image on the blue layer will be denser than the image on the red layer.

On the next page this photograph is shown as it would be recorded on each of the emulsion layers of a frame of colour film.

Transparency

Yellow image   Magenta image   Cyan image

A Negative

orange filter

Yellow image   Magenta image   Cyan image

When colour film, whether for slides or prints, is exposed to a scene containing a range of different colours, black and white negative images are formed in each of the film's three light-sensitive emulsion layers. In the case of reversal film, the images in the three layers are reversed during processing to form positive images which are then coupled with coloured dyes. In the case of print film, the reversal process is not necessary, and the dyes are coupled to the original negative images.

In addition to the colour provided by the three dyed layers, colour negatives for prints also possess an orange cast necessary to reduce contrast and correctly balance the colour dyes.

REVERSAL FILM

To understand how transparency processing works, assume that the photograph of the red cloth in our example was taken on reversal film. Since slides are viewed directly, a magenta filter and a yellow filter must be formed *right on the film's surface* if a red image is to be ultimately created from white light. This process, known as *colour reversal*, occurs on the surface of the film in what can be thought of as four stages. *Stage 1:* The latent image in the red layer of the film is developed using standard black and white processing techniques. Since no latent image exists in the blue-sensitive and green-sensitive emulsion layers at this point, they are left unchanged by the developer and remain sensitive to light. *Stage 2:* By intentionally exposing the film to white light (or to chemicals which have that effect), two black and white latent images which are identical to the *developed* image are produced, one image in the blue-sensitive layer and one in the green-sensitive layer of the film. This leaves a developed black and white image in the red layer and identical, but as yet *undeveloped*, black and white images in the blue and green layers. *Stage 3:* The black and white latent images in the blue and green layers are developed and are simultaneously *coupled* chemically with colour dyes. The developed image in the blue layer is coupled with yellow dye, and the developed image in the green layer is coupled with magenta dye. (Coupling takes place during development; there-fore, the already developed image in the red layer remains uncoupled.) *Stage 4:* The black and white images in all three layers are completely "bleached" away through the action of bleaching chemicals, leaving only the coloured dyes. The final result is a transparency consisting of a yellow filter layer and a magenta filter layer. White light projected through the slide will now be changed to red light by the subtractive action of the filters, thereby reproducing the original colour of the scene.

Print film

Assume now that the red cloth in our example was photographed not on slide film but on print film. With prints, the film itself is not viewed directly but instead is used to form a colour image on a separate sheet of printing paper, which itself is coated with three light-sensitive emulsion layers. As a result, the black and white processing step used in the first stage of developing reversal film is unnecessary because no additional latent images need to be produced on other layers of the film. Instead, the film needs to be prepared during processing so that it can later be used to produce magenta and yellow filter layers in the emulsions on the printing paper. Therefore, during initial development of the film, the latent image present in the red-sensitive layer in our example is coupled immediately with *cyan* dye. Thereafter, the developed black and white image on the film is bleached away, and the other two emulsion layers are chemically eliminated, so all that remains on the final film is a single cyan image.

Since cyan filters pass blue and green light but block red light, the cyan-dyed film when placed in an enlarger serves as a means of producing latent images in both the blue-sensitive and green-sensitive emulsions layered onto a colour printing paper's surface. Once these latent images are formed on the printing paper, the procedures for processing the print are very similar to those used for processing transparencies. During development of the latent images, yellow dye is chemically coupled with the black and white image in the blue layer, and magenta dye is coupled with the black and white image in the green layer. (Because cyan light does not affect the red-sensitive emulsion layer on the paper, the red-sensitive emulsion is removed during the course of processing). Again through the mechanism of colour subtraction, light (from a lamp, for example) shining through the magenta and yellow filter layers on the paper reflects off the white paper backing and ends up as red light.

The basic principles of transparency and print processing remain the same regardless of the colour that hits the film — all that changes are the specific filter layers ultimately produced and their relative intensities. Colours other than pure blue, pure green, and pure red generate latent images on more than one emulsion layer, but the net effect after all processing is completed remains the same: filter layers are created to reproduce from white light the colours originally present in a scene.

PROCESSING COLOUR FILM

Colour processing kits are usually packaged
with all the chemistry you need for
processing between 6 and 16 rolls of film,
depending on the product. Some kits feature
fewer steps, easier temperature control, or
longer shelf life than others, but most
products will produce good results if you are
willing to follow the manufacturer's
instructions scrupulously.

WHAT YOU NEED

Processing colour film requires only a few more items of equipment than are necessary for processing black and white film. The chief difference is that the colour process is less likely to forgive any errors you make.

Before you begin processing the film, make certain you have the following items on hand.

Photographic thermometer

Temperature is critical and in some cases must be maintained within a range of $\pm\frac{1}{8}$°C ($\pm\frac{1}{4}$°F).

Water bath

An easy way to stabilize colour chemistry at the proper temperature is to immerse all chemicals in a temperature-adjusted water bath. Any watertight household dish will work as long as it is large enough to accommodate all the containers (including the developing tank) for the process you are using and is deep enough to provide a water level close to the level of liquids within the containers.

Bottles and measuring containers

You will need a separate bottle for each chemical used in a process and measuring containers suitable for the volumes of liquid you will be dispensing. Plastic bottles work best because they can be squeezed to eliminate air. Colour chemicals have a very short shelf life when stored in partially filled containers.

Stirring rods and funnels

You will need stirring rods and funnels for mixing and pouring.

Timing device

A stopwatch or regular darkroom timer will work well. To eliminate fumbling around during processing, "programmable" timers which can be preset to time an entire sequence of steps are also available.

Developing tank and reels

The same tanks and reels used for black and white processing are suitable for colour processing. Remember that when only one roll of film is being processed in a tank designed to hold two rolls, you need to include an empty reel *on top of* the loaded reel. (This prevents over-agitation by keeping the film reel stationary.) If you plan to submerge the tank in a water bath, choose a tank that is waterproof.

Changing bag

If you do not have a darkroom, a changing bag (available from photographic dealers) will provide sufficient darkness to enable you to transfer the film safely into the developing tank.

Colour chemistry

Chemicals are usually sold as complete kits. You can use the chemistry recommended on the instruction sheet packaged with the film or one of the independent makes which are cheaper and give excellent results. The most popular chemicals are discussed in detail on the following pages.

Precise temperature control is important in colour processing and thermometers can vary between makes. The latest type gives a digital read-out which is accurate to within plus or minus $\frac{1}{2}$° Centigrade. It is also virtually unbreakable and can be used for stirring as well.

THE COLOUR PROCESSING SET-UP

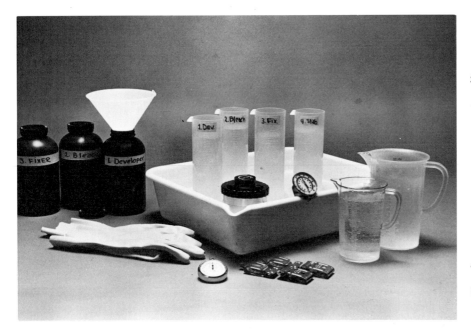

SET-UP FOR PROCESSING COLOUR FILM
1. Bottles of chemicals mixed according to the manufacturer's instructions
2. Funnel
3. Measured amounts of chemicals in a temperature controlled water bath
4. Jugs of hot and cold water for maintaining correct bath temperature
5. Thermometer
6. Processing tank in temperature-control bath
7. Protective rubber gloves
8. Stopwatch or timer
9. Clips with which to hang processed film

CONTROLLING WATER-BATH TEMPERATURE

In many colour processes it is extremely important to maintain chemicals within a narrow temperature range by keeping them in a water bath that has been warmed to the specified temperature. Since water cools during the processing procedure, you should keep on hand a container of very hot water to add to the bath as necessary to bring the temperature back up when it falls. (A container of ice water kept nearby will be useful in case you accidentally raise the temperature too high.

Be sure to return the processing tank to the water bath as often as possible in order to maintain the proper temperature of the chemicals inside.

Discipline yourself to perform the following steps each and every time you begin a colour process.

1. *Lay out materials carefully.* Make certain every item you will need is located within easy reach. Develop a consistent placement pattern to eliminate fumbling during a procedure.
2. *Pre-measure needed chemicals.* (Be certain your chemicals have not exceeded their shelf lives.) Avoid later mistakes by pouring the correct volume of each chemical into a *label-led* pouring container that you have numbered in the sequence in which you will need it. Measure out enough of each chemical to *fill the tank*, not simply to cover the reel.
3. *Prepare temperature-control water bath.* Fill the water bath dish with water that is at the correct temperature. If the chemicals need to be warmed to a temperature well above that of the room, the water you use should initially be a few degrees warmer than the temperature required. Adjust the bath temperature as necessary by adding hot water or ice water. (A plastic bag filled with ice can be placed in the bath and then removed when the temperature drops sufficiently.)
4. *Place chemical containers in water bath.*
5. *Check temperature of each chemical.* Swirl each chemical around with the thermometer as you take your readings. (*Caution:* Thoroughly clean the thermometer between chemicals to prevent contamination of one chemical by another.) Continue to monitor the chemicals and water bath until all have stabilized at the correct temperature.
6. *Prepare container of very hot water.* As the temperature of the water drops during processing, you can add hot water as needed. (This is not necessary when the recommended processing temperature is near room temperature.)
7. *Study instructions.* Be certain you understand the procedures you will have to perform. Especially important are the points below.
   a. *Determine proper agitation method.* Proper agitation is as critical as proper temperature. Use the agitation technique illustrated here unless the instructions packaged with the chemicals specify otherwise. Be absolutely certain before you begin that you know how often to agitate and for how long.
   b. *Calculate proper development time.* Depending on the process you are using, development time may need to be increased based upon the number of rolls already processed in the chemistry. The

manufacturer's instructions will tell you exactly how to calculate the correct development time. A "practice run" performed without film and using water instead of actual chemicals will reveal any steps that may be unclear to you.

c. *Place step by step outline of process close at hand.* Should the process you are using not be covered in detail here, prepare your own outline from the manufacturer's instruction sheet.

Once you have the chemicals at the correct temperature, the film loaded in the tank, the equipment laid out, the timer set, and your gloves on, you are ready to begin. Specific instructions for individual chemistries are given in the following pages, but first, here are some general rules that apply to all processes.

1. *Timing.* Begin timing the process when you start to pour chemicals into the processing tank. Begin pouring chemicals out of the tank 10–15 seconds *before* the step should be over, the exact time depending on how long it takes your tank to drain.

2. *Washing.* If you cannot use running water in the steps calling for a water wash, then fill the tank with water of the correct temperature and agitate

By keeping containers of hot and cold water close at hand, you can adjust the temperature of your water bath as necessary during the course of processing.

continuously, changing the water at least once every 30 seconds until the end of the designated washing time.

3. *Drying.* When drying colour film, do *not* wipe the emulsion side of the film. Using stabilizer in the final wash will generally produce sufficiently clean film. If you must wipe the film, gently apply soft sponges only to the non-emulsion side. To prevent water spots use stabilizers, even with kits that indicate it as optional.

AGITATION
Before you begin any process, be certain that you know how often to agitate and for how long. The basic technique discussed on p. 51 is also applicable to most colour processes.

RE-USING CHEMISTRY
In processing colour film you can usually re-use chemistry at least once, so normal procedure is to pour the used developer back into its bottle. Check the instructions prepared by the manufacturer to find out if a particular developer can be re-used as is, or if replenishment is required. (When a developer is re-used without replenishment, the developing time after the first roll or two should usually be increased.) Some kits contain two solutions of developer which require that halfway through the life of the kit you discard the first developer solution and prepare the second. The developer is the only chemical that becomes exhausted in this manner.

PROCESSING COLOUR NEGATIVES
C-41 Process

KODAK PROCESS C-41

Step	Time* min.	Temperature °C	°F	Type of Agitation
1. Developer	3¼**	37.8 ± .15	100 ± ¼	initial 30 sec. then 2 sec. every 15-sec. period.
2. Bleach	6½	24–40.5	75–105	initial 30 sec. then 5 sec. in every 30-sec. period
Remaining steps can be done under normal room light				
3. Wash	3¼	24–40.5	75–105	running water
4. Fixer	6½	24–40.5	75–105	initial 30 sec. then 5 secs. in every 30-sec. period
5. Wash	3¼	24–40.5	75–105	running water
6. Stabilizer	1½	24–40.5	75–105	initial 30 sec. only
7. Dry	usually 10–20 min.	24–43.5	75–110	

*Start timing as soon as the chemistry is poured. Allow 10 seconds to pour out chemicals.

**This time increases as the developer is exhausted. See the section "Development time compensation" in the instructions packaged with your kit for the type of film you are processing.

PHOTOCOLOR II
This British made chemistry is equally efficient and much cheaper. It uses only two baths, it can be used at much lower temperatures and total processing time is 14 minutes at 100°F (38°C).

FILM PROCESSING. Typical processing procedure at 100°F (38°C).

Pre-heat (if necessary)	1 minute
Development	3¼ minutes
Stop bath	½ minute
Bleach fix	4 minutes
Wash	5 minutes

Processing can be carried out at any temperature between 30°C (86°F) to 40°C (104°F). Full details are given in the comprehensive processing manual supplied with the kit. Solutions not used can be employed to make colour prints.

Note: If you have never before processed colour film, study the step by step photographs for E-6 processing which commence on p. 98. Although the C-41 and E-6 processes differ with respect to specific details, their underlying techniques are the same.

KODAK FLEXICOLOR PROCESSING KIT PROCESS C-41

Use. This kit is suitable for any negative film calling for C-41 processing, including Kodacolor II, Kodacolor 400, Kodak Vericolor II, Fujicolor F-II and F-II 400, Sakuracolor II and 400, Agfacolor 100, Agfacolor CNS 400, and Kodak type 5247.

Depletion compensation. Increase developing time after each roll (consult the manufacturer's instruction sheet that is included). Do not open the second bottle of developer until the first is entirely depleted or empty.

Temperature. 37.8°C ± ⅛ (100°F ± ¼).

Agitation. Agitation is especially critical due to the relatively short development time (3¼ minutes).

Total processing time. 24¼ minutes.

Special instructions. Prepare and maintain the water bath temperature at 38°C (100.5°F) if there is a large difference between room temperature and the chemical temperature. Read the warnings in the manufacturer's instruction sheet. Save all chemicals.

STEP BY STEP

Development
1. *Load film in tank* (do this in complete darkness).
2. *Set timer* for 3¼ minutes plus depletion compensation time. (Be sure to compensate for partially depleted developer, if necessary.)
3. *Check temperatures:* 37.8°C ± ¼ (100°F ± ¼).
4. *Pour developer into tank. Start timer.*
5. *Tap tank* to dislodge any air bubbles.
6. *Agitate continuously* for 30 seconds (over and back, once per second).
7. *Agitate intermittently* thereafter for the last 2 seconds of every 15-second interval until time is up, replacing the tank in the water bath between agitations.
8. *Drain tank*, pouring the developer back into its container, starting 10 seconds before the developing time is up.

Bleaching
9. *Set timer* for 6½ minutes.
10. *Pour bleach into tank. Start timer.*
11. *Agitate continuously* for 30 seconds (over and back, once per second).

12. *Agitate intermittently* thereafter for the last 5 seconds of every 30-second interval.
13. *Drain tank*, pouring the bleach back into its container, starting 10 seconds before the bleaching time is up.

Washing (from this phase on, light will not affect the film)
14. *Set timer* for 3¼ minutes.
15. *Start timer.*
16. *Wash film* in running water at 38°C (100°F).
17. *Empty water from tank* after 3¼ minutes.

Fixing

18. *Set timer* for 6½ minutes.
19. *Pour fixer into tank. Start timer.*
20. *Agitate continuously* for 30 seconds (over and back, once per second).
21. *Agitate intermittently* for the last 5 seconds of every 30-second interval, replacing the tank in the water bath between agitations.
22. *Drain tank*, pouring the fixer back into its container starting 10 seconds before fixing time is up.

Washing

23. *Set timer* for 3¼ minutes.
24. *Start timer.*
25. *Wash film* in running water at 38°C (100°F).
26. *Empty water from tank* after 3¼ minutes.

Stabilizing

27. *Set timer* for 1½ minutes.
28. *Pour stabilizer into tank. Start timer.*
29. *Agitate continuously* but gently for 30 seconds.
30. *Place tank in water bath* and leave it there.
31. *Drain tank*, pouring the stabilizer back into its container starting 10 seconds before stabilizing time is up.

Drying

32. *Hang film to dry* in a dust-free area no warmer than 43°C (110°F) (10–20 minutes is usually sufficient). Do not squeegee the film.
33. *Remove water spots* by carefully wiping the film with a sponge moistened with stabilizer. Wipe *only* the non-emulsion side of the film. (Spotting can be minimized if the stabilizer solution used is mixed in distilled water.)

Kodak C-41 Flexicolor colour negative processing kit

PROCESSING COLOUR NEGATIVES
Unicolor K2/Total Color

Unicolor K2 colour negative processing kit.

Unicolor Total Color for processing negatives as well as prints with the same chemistry. Both boxes are necessary for processing.

UNICOLOR K2
UNICOLOR TOTAL COLOR

Use. These products are used for processing colour negative film. (The Total Color unit can also process colour prints.)

As a general rule, you will obtain the highest quality results if you develop your film in the chemistry produced or recommended by the film's manufacturer. However, alternative chemistries are available with such advantages as lower processing temperatures, fewer chemicals to mix, shorter processing times, longer shelf lives, and greater economy — advantages that may sufficiently appeal to you to compensate for somewhat diminished quality.

Processing alternative chemistries
The individual steps and chemicals may vary from process to process, but the fundamentals will remain essentially the same. For example, the techniques of tank agitation and film drying are consistent in all processes. If you study the step-by-step instructions for the Kodak C-41 process, you will be well prepared to tackle any of the alternative chemistries described here.

Depletion compensation. Add 15 seconds to the developing time for a second roll and 30 seconds for a third roll, in each 8 oz working solution.

Temperature. 38°C (100°F) for the developer step, 35–41°C (95–105°F) for the remaining steps.

Total processing time. $12\frac{3}{4}$ minutes.

Comments. K2 and Total Color differ only in that K2 comes as a kit and is used extensively for developing film. Total Color comes as a pre-mixed concentrate and can be used for both developing film and processing prints. Both K2 and Total Color have especially short processing times, and both can be prepared in small quantities, if desired. Total Color's ability to be reused to process prints makes it economical for processing limited quantities of film and prints. (Note: Chemistry that is used to process prints *cannot* then be used to develop film.)

Note: If you have never before processed colour film, study the step-by-step photographs for E-6 processing which commence on p. 100. Although the processes differ with respect to specific details, the underlying techniques involved are the same.

K2 AND TOTAL COLOR

Step	Time* Min.	Temp. °F	°C	Agitation
1. Developer†	3¼	100	38	Continuously for first 30 sec. for Total Color (15 sec. for K2), then 2-3 sec. each 15 sec. thereafter
2. Blix	6	95-105	35-41	

Remaining steps can be done with normal room lights

3. Wash	3	95-105	35-41	Running water
4. Stabilizer	½	Room temperature		

* Developing times should be increased after the first roll in the same developer. See instructions packaged with chemistry.

† For all films but Fujicolor II which start with a developing time of 3 minutes.

Colour chemicals deteriorate quickly unless air is excluded from them. These 'concertina' bottles help to preserve them after mixing.

PROCESSING COLOUR NEGATIVES
Photocolor 11

PHOTOCOLOR 11

Use. This kit is for processing all type 2 colour negative films and it can also be used for colour printing. It is suitable for Agfacolor 100, Agfacolor CNS, Kodacolor 11, Kodacolor 400, Kodak Vericolor 11, Fujicolor 1, Fujicolor , Sakuracolor 11, Sakuracolor 400, 3M's and all "own name" brands designed for processing by Kodak's C-41 process.

It is very economical and a 500 ml kit will develop at least five 35 mm or 120 roll films, while the bleach-fix solution lasts for even more.

Temperature. 38°C (100°F) is recommended but excellent results can be obtained down to 30°C (86°F) with extended development times.

Total processing time. 12¾ minutes at 38°C (100°F) which includes washing but not pre-heating the tank if this is required. Times are slightly longer for 400 ASA/ISO films and for lower temperatures.

Comment. This is a simple process consisting of just three baths – developer, stop bath and bleach-fix. A rinse in water

can be used instead of a stop bath but any proprietary stop bath, such as Photo Technology's Indicol, ensures cleanliness and arrests development instantly as well as preventing carry over of developer into the bleach-fix. No stop bath is included in the kit but it is very economical to buy and use.

Photocolor 11 is easy to mix because the chemicals are in liquid form and no powder mixing is involved. It also has excellent keeping qualities and any solution not used for film development can be used for colour printing with the addition of an additive supplied with the kit.

TABLE OF PROCESSING TIMES FOR PHOTOCOLOR 11

Stage	Time	Temperature	Notes
Preheat tank	1 min.	2°C above intended processing temperature e.g. 40°C when developing at 38°C	
Development	3¼ min.	38°C (100°F)	Or as given by diagram below
Stop Bath or Rinse	½ min.	38°C (100°F) or chosen processing temperature	
Bleach Fix	4 min. 6 min.	35-40°C (95-104°F) 30-35°C (86-95°F)	Films other than 400 ASA/ISO
	6 min. 9 min.	35-40°C (95-104°F) 30-35°C (86-95°F)	400 ASA/ISO films
Wash	5 min	30-35°C (86-95°F)	Minimum in running water or frequent changes

Agitate continuously for the first 20 seconds in the developer and tap the tank sharply to dislodge air bubbles. Afterwards agitate for 5 seconds (2 inversions) every 15 seconds.

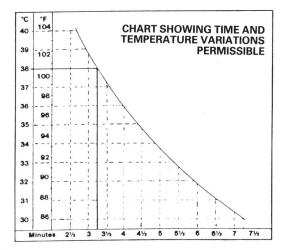

CHART SHOWING TIME AND TEMPERATURE VARIATIONS PERMISSIBLE

PROCESSING CHROMOGENIC FILMS IN PHOTOCOLOR II

These films, Ilford XP1 400 and Agfa Vario XL, can be processed in Photocolor II and this is a summary of the processing at 38°C (100°F).

Stage	Time	Temperature	Notes
Development	4 min.	38°C (100°F).	XP1 exposed at 400 ASA/ISO Vario XL exposed at 400-1600 ASA/ISO
	6 min.	38°C (100°F)	XP1 exposed at 800 ASA/ISO Vario XL, for maximum speed
	8 min	38°C (100°F)	XP1 exposed at 1600 ASA/ISO
Bleach Fix	6 min.	38° C (100°F)	
Wash	3 min.	35-40°C (95-104°F)	

Ilford XP1 developed for 4 minutes at 38°C (100°F) gives similar speed and contrast to a normal 400 ASA/ISO negative film; the developing time can be varied (say) ½ minute in either direction to suit subject contrast, individual preference, etc. Higher speed (and contrast) are obtained by increasing the developing time to 6 minutes (800 ASA/ISO) or 8 minutes (1600 ASA/ISO).

The image is red-brown in colour and the processed film has a milky appearance until dry.

Vario XL developed at 4 minutes at 38°C (100°F) gives almost its maximum speed and may be exposed at any speed from 400 to 1600 ASA/ISO – exposure at 400 ASA/ISO giving denser negatives but with excellent gradation and finer grain. Increased development has little effect except to increase fog and grain but where maximum speed is essential the developing time may be increased up to 6 minutes at 38°C (100°F).

The image is grey with a reddish tinge; the processed film also has a milky appearance until dry.

PROCESSING COLOUR TRANSPARENCIES
Kodak E-6 Process

E-6 Processing Kit

Once a roll of reversal film has been developed and dried, it can be viewed and evaluated immediately. Negative film, however, requires that the image on a frame be transferred onto printing paper before the image can be accurately evaluated. Since exposing and processing prints entails complex skills, most people prefer to learn first how to develop reversal film and then apply that knowledge to negative film. Also, most people seem to find it easier to learn how to make prints from slides than from negatives, even though the fundamental principles for both are the same. Therefore, E-6 film processing is presented below in great detail.

THE E-6 PROCESS

Kodak's E-6 processing kit is sold in two sizes: 1 pint and 1 gallon. The pint size (shown here) will process eight 36-exposure rolls of Ektachrome, or twelve 20-exposure rolls. The entire chemistry is liquid, which makes it easy to mix; the reversal process is accomplished by chemicals rather than light. Total processing time (not including drying) is 37 minutes.

The kit consists of seven chemicals with shelf lives varying from one week to twenty-four weeks, once mixed. The first developer and the colour developer are supplied in two sets to extend the life of the kit. Do not mix the second set until you have exhausted the first.

If E-6 chemistry becomes contaminated, even slightly, uneven colour will result. Therefore, take care to keep all mixing and storage containers clean. Be especially careful not to contaminate the first developer, reversal bath, or colour developer with the fixer, or to contaminate the first developer with the reversal bath. Also, keep the first and colour developers separated.

Proper agitation and temperature control are especially important. Read the instructions carefully because the agitation method required varies with the chemical used. Although the chemicals in some steps only need to be maintained within a 10–12°C (50–54°F) temperature range, try to keep the temperatures of all the chemicals as close to each other as possible.

KODAK PROCESS E-6

Step	Time min.	°C	Temp. °F	Type of Agitation	
1. First developer	7*	38	100 $\pm\frac{1}{2}$	initial 15 sec. + every 30 sec.	Total darkness
2. Wash	2	33–39	92–102		Total darkness
3. Reversal Bath	2	33–39	92–102	Initial sec. only	Total darkness

Remaining steps can be done in normal light.

Step	Time min.	°C	Temp. °F	Type of Agitation	
4. Colour developer	6	38	100 ± 2	Initial 15 sec. + every 30 sec.	
5. Conditioner	2	33–39	92–102	Initial only	
6. Bleach	7	33–39	92–102	Initial 15 sec. + every 30 sec.	
7. Fixer	4	33–39	92–102	Initial 15 sec. + every 30 sec.	
8. Wash	6	33–39	92–102		
9. Stabilizer	1	33–39	92–102	Initial 15 secs. only	
10. Dry		not over 40	104		

*Each pint of first developer can process 4 rolls of 36 exposure film. Seven minutes is used for the first 2 rolls but the time should be increased to $7\frac{1}{2}$ minutes for the second 2 rolls.

A simple water bath for temperature control which can be heated by a fishtank heater and a thermostat control is a nice extra. A paper drum, hand operated, is seen here but it can be easily adapted to take a film processing drum.

KODAK E-6 PROCESS
Step by step

THE KODAK E-6 PROCESSING KIT

Use. This kit is suitable for all Kodak Ektachrome reversal films.

Depletion compensation. Add 2 minutes to development time after two rolls have been processed.

Temperature. First developer: 37.8 $\pm\frac{1}{4}$°C (100 $\pm\frac{1}{2}$°F): colour developer: 38 $\pm$ 17°C (100 $\pm$ 2°F); other liquids: 33–39°C (92–102°F) (but try to keep all temperatures as near to each other as possible).

Total processing time. 37 minutes.

Comments. Adjust the temperature of the running water to 33–39°C (92–102°F). Be careful to keep all mixing and storage containers clean, as E-6 chemicals contaminate easily. Be especially careful to keep the fixer out of the developers and reversal bath, and the reversal bath out of the first developer. Also, keep the two developers completely separated.

FIRST DEVELOPER
1. *Set timer* to 7 minutes.
2. *Verify temperature* (38 $\pm$ 0.3°C) (100.4 $\pm\frac{1}{2}$°F). **Adjust if necessary.**
3. *Pour developer into tank. Start timer.*
4. *Tap tank.*
5. *Agitate.*
6. *Drain tank* starting 10 seconds before time is up.

WATER WASH
7. *Set timer* to 2 minutes.
8. *Verify temperature* of water (33–39°C) (92–102°F). **Adjust if necessary.**
9. *Fill tank with clean water* (33–39°C) (92–102°F). *Start timer.*
10. *Discard water then replace with clean water* continually until the timer rings.

REVERSAL BATH
11. *Set timer* to 2 minutes.
12. *Verify water temperature* (33–39°C) (92–102°F). **Adjust if necessary.**
13. *Pour reversal bath into tank. Start timer.*
14. *Tap tank.*
15. *Agitate continuously* for 1 minute.

16. *Do not agitate* for the second minute. (Remainder of the process can be completed with tank cover removed, see photograph).
17. *Drain tank* starting 10 seconds before time is up.

COLOUR DEVELOPER
18. *Set timer* to 6 minutes.
19. *Verify temperature* of colour developer (32 $\pm$ 0.6°C) (100.4 $+$ 1.1°F).
20. *Adjust temperature* if necessary.
21. *Tap tank.*
22. *Agitate.*
23. *Drain tank* starting 10 seconds before time is up.

CONDITIONER

24. *Set timer* to 2 minutes.
25. *Verify temperature* (33–39°C) (92–102°F). Adjust, if necessary.
26. *Pour conditioner in tank. Start timer.*
27. *Tap tank.*
28. *Agitate once* (over and back).
29. *Return tank to water bath.*
30. *Drain tank* starting 10 seconds before time is up.

BLEACH

31. *Set timer* to 7 minutes.
32. *Verify temperature* (33–39°C) (92–102°F). Adjust, if necessary.
33. *Pour bleach into tank. Start timer.*
34. *Tap tank.*
35. *Agitate.*
36. *Drain tank,* starting 10 seconds before time is up.

FIXER

37. *Set timer* to 4 minutes.
38. *Verify temperature* (33–39°C) (92–102°F). Adjust, if necessary.
39. *Pour fixer in tank. Start timer.*
40. *Agitate.*
41. *Drain tank* starting 10 seconds before time is up.

WATER WASH

42. *Set timer* to 6 minutes.
43. *Verify temperature of water* (33–39°C) (92–102°F).
44. *Wash film* in continuously running water.
45. *Drain tank* when time is up.

STABILIZER

46. *Set timer* to 1 minute.
47. *Pour stabilizer into tank* (its temperature is not critical).
48. *Start timer.*
49. *Agitate once.* (over and back).
50. *Replace tank in water bath.*
51. *Drain tank* starting 10 seconds before time is up.

DRYING

52. *Hang film to dry.*
53. *Wipe non-emulsion side* (optional) with sponge moistened with *stabilizer.* Do not squeegee or apply sponge to emulsion side.
54. *Remove film* when dry. Wet film has a milky blue cast which disappears when the film is completely dry.

PROCESSING COLOUR TRANSPARENCIES
Chrome-Six

Chrome-Six comes in 1 litre and 4 litre sizes. The chemicals are in liquid form so they are easy to mix and it is also possible to mix only the amounts required. The remainder will last longer if the plastic bottles are squeezed to eliminate as much air as possible.

Use. The Chrome-Six chemistry designed by the British Photo Technology Company Limited provides a simpler and more economical means of processing Ektachrome E-6 reversal film and other compatible films, such as Barfen, Fujichrome and 3M's. It should not be used for films requiring the Kodak E-4 process.

Temperature. Any temperature within the range 34°C to 42°C (93°F to 108°F) can be used with development times varied according to the chart opposite.

Processing times. Excluding washing and drying the times vary from about $25\frac{1}{2}$ minutes at 43°C (110°F) to 32 minutes at 34°C (93°F).

Comments. Only four processing solutions are required and they are made from six liquid concentrates provided with the kit. Any convenient volume of solution can be made up as required and the remainder stored for future use. The keeping qualities are good. Chrome-Six is available in 1 litre and 4 litre kits, and the solutions are in squeeze bottles with spare colour-coded caps to avoid contamination between the concentrates.

Capacity. Up to 10 films (35mm or 120 rollfilm) can be processed in 500ml with standard processing times. This makes the cost per film very economical compared with others.

Compensation. Where film has been accidentally exposed at higher or lower than the ASA/ISO rating it is possible to carry out a degree of compensation by increasing or decreasing the development times. See the table opposite.

Processing requires accurate temperature control and it is made easier with a temperature bath which keeps the revolving drum and all the chemicals at the right temperature. This model takes drums for colour paper or films and the motor drives them with a reciprocating action.

CHROME-SIX PROCESSING

Time and temperature table

First Development	6½ minutes	38°C (100°F).
		See correction diagram.
Wash	2 minutes	34–42°C (93–108°F).
Reversal Bath	2 minutes	34–42°C (93–108°F).
Colour Development	6 minutes	38° C (100°F).
		See correction diagram.
Wash	1 minute	34–42°C (93–108°F).
Bleach Fix	8 minutes	34–42°C (93–108°F).
Wash	4 minutes	34–42°C (93–108°F)
Dry		

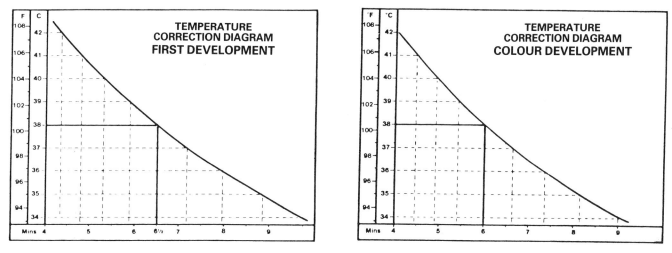

Increasing and reducing film speed

In difficult light, an emergency or where a film has been accidentally exposed at the wrong ASA/ISO rating, the speed can be reduced or increased by varying the First Developing time as follows:–

To reduce speed to about ⅓ normal
e.g. 200 ASA/ISO film exposed at 64 ASA/ISO.
Reduce First Development by ⅓.

To reduce speed to about ½ normal
e.g. 200 ASA/ISO film exposed at 100 ASA/ISO.
Reduce First Development by ⅙.

To increase speed to about 2x normal
e.g. 200 ASA/ISO film exposed at 400 ASA/ISO.
Increase First Development by ⅓.

To increase speed to about 4x normal
e.g. 200 ASA/ISO film exposed at 800 ASA/ISO.
Double First Development.

The effect varies slightly from film to film and it is advisable to make tests to establish optimum speed settings. The maximum increase obtainable is about x4 (2 stops) but it may be possible to get acceptable results with meters or automatic cameras set at even higher speeds.

Varying First Development does not affect the capacity of the solution.

Drums for 35mm and roll films which fit the processor on the opposite page by means of magnets attached to the bases. These marry a magnet on the drive shaft, thus facilitating snap-on-and-off fitting.

6. THE COLOUR PRINT

Walk into a large photographic dealer and you will be confronted with shelf after shelf of competing products, each recommended for a special set of conditions, each with its own advantages and disadvantages. No matter which chemistries you select, if you understand the fundamentals of filtration and colour printing and follow the manufacturers' processing instructions carefully, you will be assured of good results – even if you have never entered a darkroom before. Moreover, once you have a complete command of one of the processes, the others lining the store shelves will be so similar that you will easily be able to transfer the skills you have learned. Times and temperatures may change, but sequences and methods will remain essentially the same.

Think of colour printing as consisting of two stages. The first stage, *exposing the paper*, involves selecting the proper filtration and determining the correct exposure. The second stage, *processing the print*, involves the mechanical procedures of mixing chemicals and using them correctly in drums or dishes to produce a final, properly developed image.

If you have never attempted colour processing before, here is a simple, nearly foolproof strategy for learning to produce high-quality colour prints.

1. Study the concepts and procedures for determining correct filtration and exposure until you understand them thoroughly (pp. 106-109).
2. Decide whether you want to print from transparencies or negatives. (Unless you expect to be printing exclusively from negatives in the future, start with transparencies because it is far easier to visualize the effect of filtration on transparencies than on negatives. Switch to negatives later, if you wish.)
3. Select and purchase one of the chemical kits described in this chapter. It is not too important which you select as long as your selection is consistent with the type of film you want to print from, transparencies or negatives).
4. Purchase or borrow the equipment you will need.
5. Select a "practice" transparency or negative that is properly exposed, preferably contains flesh tones, and displays a variety of colours.
6. Follow the instructions on pp. 72-73 for making test prints and a final print. If the processing chemistry you have chosen is not covered in detail on the following pages, refer to the section in its manufacturer's instruction sheet that relates to your needs.
7. Continue to use the same chemistry over and over with different transparencies or negatives (as appropriate) until you have completely mastered exposure, filtration, and the manufacturer's process.
8. Eventually, try alternative chemistries that sound interesting or that allow you to switch from transparencies to negatives or vice versa.

DETERMINING FILTRATION

The first step in adjusting filtration is identifying the colour that is out of balance in your print. In most circumstances, you will find that colour imbalances are easiest to read where they affect flesh tones.

In the photograph above, the three colour-compensating filters (yellow, magenta, and cyan) have been laid over a colour transparency to illustrate how colour imbalances affect flesh tones. Study the photograph carefully until you are certain you can recognize the effect of each imbalance by sight and can correctly name the out-of-balance colour.

Note that where two filters overlap, a primary colour is formed, and where all three overlap, the area of neutral density appears darker but the actual colour of the skin remains unchanged.

UNDERSTANDING FILTRATION

In colour printing, inaccurate duplication of the original colours of a scene may occur for three reasons: inconsistencies in the light produced by different enlarger bulbs; variations in the colours present in the transparencies or negatives being used to make a print; and differences in the response of paper batches to the colours contained in light. Each time you expose a print, these three sources of colour inaccuracy combine, requiring that you use compensating filters in order to produce a print with natural colour balance.

The heart of successful colour printing is the analysing of a print to determine which colours are out of balance. Therefore, it is crucial that you spend time studying the colour chart on the next page until you can identify and name each of the six colours by sight.

Colour filters

If you recall from p. 82, there are three filters used in subtractive colour photography: yellow, magenta, and cyan. Furthermore, by stacking the filters in various combinations of two, you can generate the primary colours, blue, green, and red. Finally, stacking all three filters produces what is called a *grey or neutral density (ND) filter*; that is, a filter that has no colour but which causes light passing through it to lose intensity.

Filter density

The intensity of the colour in a filter is measured in terms of colour *density*. Dichroic heads allow you to adjust filtration in single units of density, whereas colour-printing (CP) and colour-compensating (CC) filters are commonly available in increments no smaller than 5 units. (A supply of CP or CC filters with the densities 5, 10, 20, 40, and 50 in each of the colours yellow, magenta, and cyan should satisfy your needs.) In general, 5 units represents a minor correction, 10–15 units a moderate correction, and 20 or more units a large correction; however, some papers, such as Cibachrome, require larger changes.

The filter pack

The filtration in your enlarger is referred to as a *filter pack*, whether you are using actual filters or dialling in filtration on a dichroic head. Even a brand new en-larger will have some filtration in its filter pack because of the colours generated by the enlarger's own internal components. Also, every paper batch responds differently to the colours in light. Each time you switch to a different paper batch, you must make a test print based on the manufacturer's recommended filtration and then adjust the colour as necessary by adding or removing filters from the filter pack.

Eliminating natural density

Since equal densities of three filters produce neutral density, removing equal amounts from all three filters of a filter pack will not affect the colour of the print. In other words, normally you should not expose a print if your filter pack contains all three filter colours. Instead, first eliminate the filter of lowest density and then subtract that density from the two remaining colours. For example, from a filter pack containing 5Y, 20M, and 30C, you should remove 5Y, 5M, and 5C, leaving 15M and 25C.

ADJUSTING FILTRATION

Once you have decided which colour is out of balance in a print, you must decide how to make the necessary filtration adjustment. Charts that present two alternative methods for correcting each of the six possible colour imbalances are shown on p. 111 (for printing from slides) and p. 113 (for printing from negatives). In each case, one method involves adding filters and the other subtracting them. Either method will work, but one is usually easier to use than the other depending on which filters are already in the filter pack. Here is a useful procedure for making the adjustment.

1. Remove any neutral density from the filter pack.
2. Consult the appropriate chart (pp. 111 or 112) to determine the two filtration options you have.
3. If possible, select the option that permits you to work with the colours already in your filter pack.

If step 3 requires you to subtract more of a colour than is already present in the filter pack, then do the following:

4. Use the additive option instead.
5. Remove any neutral density that is formed.

For example, suppose that when printing from a transparency, you determine that the test print contains far too much magenta. From the chart on p. 111, you will see that you can solve the problem either by subtracting magenta or by adding yellow and cyan. If you estimate a correction of 20 units, and your filter pack already contains 10Y and 25C, you would add 20Y and 20C, ending up with a filter pack containing 30Y and 45C.

Suppose, in the above example, that you are printing from a negative instead of a transparency. In that case, from the chart on p. 112 you see that you can remove magenta from the print by *adding* magenta to the filter pack or by *subtracting* cyan and yellow. However, because you cannot subtract 20Y from a filter pack containing only 10Y, you must elect to add 20M, producing a filter pack which contains 10Y, 20M, and 25C. Removing 10 units of neutral density, your final filter pack ends up with 10M and 15C.

Filter exposure compensations

Whenever you change the amount of filtration you use with a condenser-head enlarger, exposure also changes. If you *add* filters, to find the new exposure time *multiply* your standard exposure (see p. 108) time by the appropriate factor given in the chart below. If you *subtract* filters, *divide* your exposure time by the appropriate factor. For changes involving two filters, first multiply the respective filter factors together, then proceed as described above. Each time you add or subtract filters, you must make an additional exposure compensation.

	Y	M	C
5	1.1	1.2	1.1
10	1.1	1.3	1.2
20	1.1	1.5	1.3
30	1.1	1.7	1.4
40	1.1	1.9	1.5
50	1.1	2.1	1.6

THE COLOUR WHEEL IN TERMS OF NEUTRAL DENSITY

Red is Yellow *plus* Magenta

RED
Red is Neutral Density *minus* Cyan

MAGENTA

YELLOW

Neutral Density: equal amounts of the three complementary colours: yellow, magenta and cyan

Green is Cyan *plus* Yellow

GREEN
Green is Neutral Density *minus* Magenta

BLUE
Blue is Neutral Density *minus* Yellow

Blue is Magenta *plus* Cyan

CYAN

The relationship between the primary colours (blue, green, and red) and the complementary colours (yellow, magenta, and cyan) is the foundation of colour filtration. For colour printing, you will find it most useful to commit the following to memory:
1. **Magenta plus yellow produces red (M + Y = R), cyan plus magenta produces blue (C + M = B), and yellow plus cyan produces green (Y + C = G).**
2. **When all three colours are combined, neutral density (which has no colour) results.**
3. **Each primary colour can be formed** *by removing the appropriate complementary (or secondary) colour from neutral density.*

DETERMINING EXPOSURE

EXPOSING FOR PRINTS

In colour printing, improperly exposed prints suffer from unpredictable colour shifts. Therefore, your final filtration must be based on a test print that is correctly exposed.

Controlling exposure

The particular combinations of enlarger-lens f-stop and exposure duration required for a properly exposed print are dictated by four factors: the power of your enlarger lamp, the density of your transparency or negative, the size of your enlargement, and the light-sensitivity of your paper.

You can adjust exposure by changing either f-stop or exposure time. In practice, however, you will find it far easier to choose a standard exposure time and use it whenever possible, making all your exposure adjustments by changing f-stop alone. This method is favoured because some colour printing papers do not respond predictably to changes in exposure time. Changes in f-stop, on the other hand, produce completely predictable exposure changes that are consistent irrespective of the paper used.

Selecting a standard exposure time

You will greatly simplify your darkroom efforts if you establish a standard exposure time that will allow you quickly and consistently to select a correct f-stop without having to make more than one test print. Set your enlarger at f/8 and, using the paper you expect to employ most frequently, experiment to determine the exposure time that will produce a properly exposed 8″ x 10″ (20 x 25 cm) enlargement (see p. 72). The f/8 setting gives you an intermediate lens opening which will permit you to make f-stop

changes in either direction while still using your standard exposure time. This strategy facilitates finding the correct exposure for various enlargements because changing to 5″ x 7″ (13 x 18 cm) or 11″ x 14″ (28 x 36 cm) from 8″ x 10″ requires a change in exposure of exactly one f-stop, and changing to 4″ x 5″ (10 x 13 cm) or 16″ x 20″ (41 x 51 cm) requires a change of exactly two f-stops.

Selecting a test paper size

You can make a test print on paper of any size. The 4″ x 5″ size is economical to use, but 4″ x 5″ processing drums are not readily available. Some 8″ x 10″ drums will accommodate the smaller paper size, but you will still need to use as much chemistry as an 8″ x 10″ sheet requires.

Regardless of the size of your test paper, you must adjust the enlarger for your test print so that the image striking the paper is exactly the size it will be in the final print.

Making a test for exposure

Perform a test for exposure as follows:
1. *Prepare an "L" shaped mask for test paper size you have selected. (See middle photograph at top.)*

CUTTING A TESTING "L"
In an exposure test, you expose each of four quadrants of a sheet of paper at a different f-stop, then use the exposure that looks best to make the final print. A testing "L" simplifies the process of exposing one quadrant at a time.

To make a testing "L", cut a piece of cardboard to the same size as your paper, then cut out one quadrant as shown.

2. *Place slide or negative transparency or negative in enlarger,* emulsion side down.
3. *Insert (or dial in) estimated filter pack* recommended by the paper manufacturer (or one you have derived by experience).
4. *Turn of all lights* except the enlarger lamp.
5. *Adjust enlarger head* to produce the correct enlargement size.
6. *Focus at the widest f-stop.*
7. *Turn off enlarger lamp.*
8. *Place test paper on easel* (in total darkness).
9. *Place cardboard "L" on paper* so cutout is in upper left-hand corner. (See right photograph at top.)
10. *Set lens at f/16* (or the smallest f-stop your lens has).
11. *Expose paper for your standard time.*
12. *Repeat steps 8, 9, and 10 three times,* but simultaneously turn and rotate the cut-out clockwise to a different corner and open the lens by one f-stop each time.
13. *Load test print in a processing drum,* emulsion side *in.*
14. *Process print normally.* (See later sections of this chapter).

PERFORMING THE EXPOSURE TEST
When performing the exposure test, place the "L" so that one quarter of the paper is uncovered, set your lens to the smallest f-stop you will be using, then make your exposure. Next, rotate and/or turn the cardboard so that a different quadrant is uncovered, open the lens one f-stop, and make your second exposure. Repeat this process until all four quadrants have been exposed, each at a different f-stop. Finally, process the print and select the best exposure to use for your final print.

f/5.6   f/8

EXPOSURE TEST
After you have performed an exposure test, your processed test print should appear similar to the one above. In this example, the best exposure is at *f*/11. If all quarters in your test print appear over or underexposed, you must repeat the test using a different sequence of *f*-stops or changing the exposure time.

f/16   f/11

Evaluating an exposure test

Evaluate the results of an exposure test as follows:

1. *Dry print thoroughly.* Never try to judge a wet print, because colour and brightness change as a print dries.
2. *Decide which of the four exposures is best.* Often the best exposure will fall between two *f*-stops.
3. *Repeat the test* (as described below) if all four exposures are either under-exposed or overexposed, or if the filtration is grossly in error.

Repeating an exposure test

Occasionally all four exposures on your test print will be over or underexposed, in which case you must test again using a different exposure time. The procedure is as follows:

Maintaining a darkroom log

To aid you in your darkroom endeavours, you should maintain a darkroom log. Notes to yourself, problems and their solutions, ideas, comments, and the like, will prove invaluable for later reference. Because the same exposure and filter pack will almost always produce a high-quality print from any properly exposed slide or negative enlarged to the *same size* on the *same paper batch*, you will find it especially useful to include in your

log a record of the exposure and filtration data for each batch of paper you use.

1. *Determine whether you need to increase or decrease the exposure.* For prints from transparencies, increasing the amount of light falling on the paper *lightens* the print, and vice versa. For prints from negatives, increasing the amount of light falling on the paper *darkens* the prints, and vice versa.
2. *Select a different exposure time.* If you must increase the exposure time, do so by more than double. If you must decrease the exposure time, do so by more than half.
3. Repeat the entire test procedure at the new exposure time.

Making a filtration test

If the properly exposed quarter of your exposure test reveals that your filtration is off, you may want to estimate the filtration correction and then perform a separate filtration test, unless you are confident that your estimated correction will be accurate. The advantage of a test is that you can do it on a small piece of printing paper. You do not need to use the testing "L" because you only need to make a single exposure at the correct *f*-stop.

COLOUR PRINTING FROM TRANSPARENCIES

Paper types

The two papers most widely available for making colour prints directly from transparencies are Kodak Ektachrome RC14 paper and Cibachrome paper. Type RC14 can be processed in Kodak chemistry or in chemistries such as Photochrome-R produced by other manufacturers. However, no manufacturer other than Cibachrome makes chemistry designed specifically for use with Cibachrome paper. You will achieve high quality results if you use the paper manufacturer's own chemistry or one of the reputable brands.

Exposures

Cibachrome recommends that you make exposure adjustments by changing lens openings while keeping exposure time constant, whereas Kodak recommends altering exposure time instead. However, if you follow the procedures for determining a standard exposure time suggested on p. 108 you can adjust exposure by changing lens opening with either paper.

Exposure and filtration corrections

Exposure and filtration corrections are easier with transparencies than with negatives because corrections seem intuitively logical. For example, if a print is too dark, you lighten it by using a larger *f*-stop, thereby increasing the amount of light striking the paper, and if the print displays too much of a colour, you subtract that colour from the enlarger's filter pack.

1. *Clean transparency* thoroughly.
2. *Place transparency in enlarger,* emulsion side down (i.e. facing the easel).

6. *Position easel* to crop the print where you wish.
7. *Close down aperture* to the exposure setting as determined by your test exposures.
8. *Turn off enlarger lamp*
●9. *Place paper on easel* without changing the easel's position.
●10. *Expose* paper for the standard time interval (or a special interval as determined by your test exposures).

3. *Insert (or dial in) filter pack* as determined from your test prints.
4. *Turn off all lights* except the enlarger lamp.
5. *Adjust focus* with the lens set at its widest *f*-stop.

●11. *Load paper* in processing drum, emulsion side *in.*
●12. *Cap ends of drum.*
13. *Turn lights on.*
14. *Process print.*

Execute steps preceded by a "●" in complete darkness.

110

The two illustrations and their accompanying captions on this page will serve as a guide to making exposure and filtration decisions. (Remember not to judge a print until it is dry.)

Printing from a transparency

In order to make a final print from a transparency, you need to have (1) decided on the size of enlargement you want to make, (2) made an exposure test, (3) determined the best exposure setting, and (4) calculated the adjustments to make in your enlarger's filter pack to correct any colour imbalances. Once these preliminaries have been completed, follow the steps outlined in the captions at right to produce your final print.

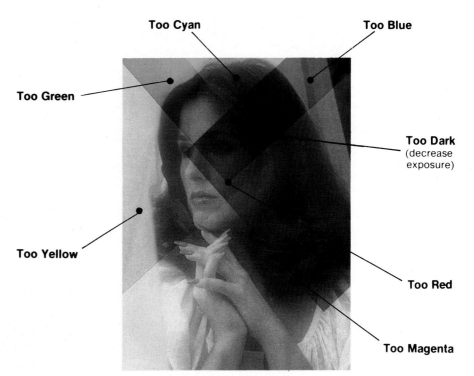

Too Cyan   **Too Blue**
Too Green
Too Dark
(decrease exposure)
Too Yellow
Too Red
Too Magenta

 f/5.6   f/8

f/16   f/11

ADJUSTING THE COLOUR FILTRATION WITH TRANSPARENCIES
The above photograph shows various colour errors and the filters that produce them. Errors show up most clearly in flesh tones. You correct colour errors in prints made from transparencies by *subtracting* from the filter pack the colour that contributes to the error, or by *adding* its complementary colour (see chart below). Be sure to remove any neutral density that your corrections produce in the filter pack (see p. 107).

If you do not know how large a correction to make, start with a filter density correction of 20 units. (Viewing aids, which are discussed on p. 116, will help you to estimate the corrections necessary.

SELECTING THE LENS APERTURE
In the sample test print shown at left, the exposure at *f*/16 seems too dark and the one at *f*/8 seems too light, so so for the final print you would set the enlarger aperture to *f*/11.

If all four quarters of your test print appear too light, you must repeat the test using an exposure time *less* than half as long (4 seconds instead of 10 seconds, for example). If all four quarters of your test print appear too dark, repeat the test using an exposure time *more* than twice as long (25 seconds instead of 10 seconds, for example).

Adjusting Colour Filtration with Transparencies

If your print is too	Then subtract	Or add
Blue	Magenta + Cyan	Yellow
Green	Yellow + Cyan	Magenta
Red	Yellow + Magenta	Cyan
Yellow	Yellow	Magenta + Cyan
Magenta	Magenta	Yellow + Cyan
Cyan	Cyan	Yellow + Magenta

COLOUR PRINTING FROM NEGATIVES

SELECTING A LENS OPENING
In the sample test print shown on p. 111 the exposure at *f*/16 seems too dark while the one at *f*/5.6 seems too light. For the final print, you would set the enlarger between *f*/8 and *f*/11.

If all four quarters of your test print appear too light, you must repeat the test using an exposure time *more* than twice as long (20 seconds instead of 8 seconds, for example). If all four quarters of your test print appear too dark, repeat the test using an exposure *less* than half as long (3 seconds instead of 8 seconds, for example).

Colour negatives, unlike transparencies, bear no apparent colour resemblance to the prints they produce. Moreover, the negatives contain an orange cast designed to reduce contrast in the final print. The orange cast in no way interferes with colour rendition but since the film contains a negative rather than a positive image, the cast makes it difficult to evaluate the quality of a negative without actually making a print.

Printing from colour negatives requires that you produce a contact print of each roll of film so that you can evaluate the individual frames on the roll and decide which frames you want to enlarge. The dilemma is that in order to produce a contact, you must first know how to make a print; but in order to select a good negative, you first need to make a contact. Therefore, you need to be familiar with the information on this page as well as on the following two pages before you begin printing.

Paper types
The most readily available and widely used papers for printing from colour negatives are Kodak Ektacolor 74RC and Photocolor papers. These papers are sold in two surface textures. The type you use is a matter of personal preference.

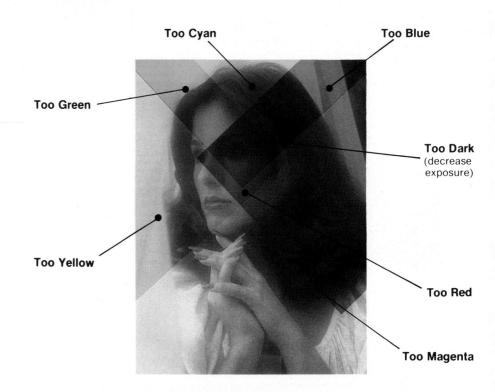

ADJUSTING COLOUR FILTRATION WITH NEGATIVES
The above photograph shows various colour errors and the filters that produce them. Errors show up most clearly in flesh tones. You correct colour errors in prints made from negatives by *adding* to the filter pack the colour that contributes to the error by *removing* its complementary colour (see chart below). Be sure to remove any neutral density that your corrections produce in the filter pack (see p. 105).

If you do not know how large a correction to make, start with a filter density correction of 20 units. (Viewing aids, which are discussed on p. 114 will help you estimate corrections.)

Adjusting Colour Filtration With Negatives

If your print is too:	Then add	Or subtract
Blue	Magenta + Cyan	Yellow
Green	Yellow + Cyan	Magenta
Red	Yellow + Magenta	Cyan
Yellow	Yellow	Magenta + Cyan
Magenta	Magenta	Yellow + Cyan
Cyan	Cyan	Yellow + Magenta

You will achieve the highest quality results with these papers if you process them in Kodak Ektaprint 2 or Photocolor II chemistry. However, alternative chemistries are also available.

Exposure and filtration correction

The effects of changes in exposure and filtration when printing from colour negatives are exactly the opposite of what you would logically expect. If a test print is too dark, you must *decrease* the exposure to lighten the print, and vice versa. If a test print displays too much of a colour, you *add* that colour to the enlarger's filter pack; if you need to add a colour to the print, you subtract that colour from the filter pack.

The two illustrations on this page will serve as a guide for making exposure and filtration decisions. As always, remember not to judge a print's colour until it is dry.

Printing from a negative

In order to make a final print from a negative, you need to have (1) made a contact print and selected a frame to enlarge, (2) decided on the enlargement size you want, (3) made a test exposure, p. 108, (4) determined the best exposure setting, and (5) calculated the adjustments to make in your enlarger's filter pack to correct any colour imbalance (this page).

Once you have completed these preliminaries, follow the steps outlined in the captions on the previous page to produce your final print.

INTERNEGATIVES

Background

In the early days of colour printing, reversal printing papers produced a substantial increase in contrast, so transparencies were copied onto negative film (thereby producing an internegative) which was then used to make a print on standard negative-to-positive paper. Today, reversal papers are so vastly improved that the slightly better contrast possible with negative paper does not compensate for the loss in image quality produced by generating an internegative.

Printing from internegatives

To produce an internegative, load your camera with negative film and then follow the procedures described on p. 136 for slide copying. Then make your print by following the normal procedures for printing from a negative.

STEP BY STEP
1. *Clean negative thoroughly.*
2. *Place negative in enlarger, emulsion side down (i.e., facing the baseboard).*

3. *Insert (or dial in) filter pack as determined from your test prints.*
4. *Turn off all lights except the enlarger lamp.*
5. *Adjust focus with the lens set at its widest f-stop.*

6. *Position easel so as to crop the print where you wish.*
7. *Close down aperture to the exposure setting determined by your test exposures.*
8. *Turn off enlarger lamp.*
9. *Place paper in masking frame or on baseboard.*
10. *Expose paper for the standard time interval (or a special interval as determined by your test exposures).*

11. *Load paper in processing drum, emulsion side in.*
12. *Cap ends of drum.*
13. *Turn lights on.*
14. *Process print.*

Execute steps preceded by a " • " in complete darkness.

COLOUR CONTACT PRINTS

CONTACT PRINTING

Before you can make a satisfactory contact print of a roll of negative film, you must determine the correct filtration for the paper you are using and the correct exposure for an 8″ x 10″ enlargement. Once you know these figures, they will be applicable any time you make a contact using the same paper batch. Be sure to make a note in your darkroom log of the height of the enlarger head above the baseboard, as well as the exposure and filter-pack values.

Test frames

You can use any properly exposed negative as a test frame, but you will obtain the best results if your test frame contains flesh tones and a broad range of colours. An excellent technique is to prepare your own special test frame consisting of a portrait of a person holding up a standard colour chart (colour charts are available from photographic dealers). Save the test frame and use it whenever you use a new paper batch.

Contact printer

The same contact printers used for black and white photography are suitable for colour.

Making the contact

Once you have established the correct exposure for an 8″ x 10″ enlargement and the correct filter pack for the paper batch you are using, follow the steps outlined in the captions on this page to produce your final print.

Execute steps preceded by a "●" in complete darkness.

CONTACT PRINTING
1. *Adjust enlarger* to the proper height for the light to cover an 8″ x 10″ (20 x 25 cm) sheet of paper.
2. *Set correct lens opening* as determined from your test prints.

3. *Set timer.*
4. *Insert (or dial in) correct filter pack* for the paper batch being used.
5. *Turn off all lights.*

● 6. *Insert 8″ × 10″ paper in contact printer, emulsion side up.*
● 7. *Place negatives on top of paper, emulsion side down.*
● 8. *Close contact printer.*
● 9. *Position contact printer directly below the enlarger lens.*

● 10. *Expose paper for the standard time interval.*
● 11. *Load paper in processing drum, emulsion side in*
● 12. *Cap ends of drum.*
13. *Turn lights on.*
14. *Process print.*

BLACK AND WHITE FROM COLOUR

BLACK AND WHITE PRINTS FROM COLOUR ORIGINALS

On occasion you may find you have a colour negative that you would like to print in black and white. Special papers enable you to do so.

Paper

Since normal black and white printing paper does not respond to all colours, you cannot use it to print from a colour negative because some colours present in the original will not show up in the print. Kodak Panalure paper, however, which comes in F (glossy) and E (lustre) surfaces, is sensitive to all colours and is suitable for producing a black and white image from a colour original.

Safelights

Panalure's sensitivity to all colours makes the use of a safelight risky. Kodak says you can use a grade 10 amber filter with a 15-watt bulb at no closer than 4 ft for brief periods, but you are safest exposing the paper to no extraneous light at all until processing is completed.

Filtration

Filters have the same effect on Panalure paper as on black and white film. For example, if you want to darken the sky in a print, you can hold a medium yellow or red filter below the enlarger lens as you make the exposure.

Processing

You process Panalure paper using standard black and white processing procedures, except that without having the visibility provided by a safelight, you will have to use an audible timer to determine when developing is completed.

Image quality suffers when normal black and white paper is used to make a print from a colour negative. Notice how the above photograph has become "contrasty", in that detail has been lost in the shadows (especially in the man's face) and in the highlights (the large rock). Also, the print shows increased grain.

Black and white papers specifically intended for use with colour negatives preserve image quality. Because these papers are designed to respond to all colours in the spectrum, contrast remains substantially the same; on the other hand, no safelight can be used. Grain, like contrast, remains within acceptable levels.

COLOUR PRINTING AIDS

COLOUR CALCULATOR

Colour calculators work by blending together all the colours in a transparency or negative, then projecting the mixture through a wide range of different filter combinations and densities onto a sheet of printing paper. The filter combination that produces a neutral grey colour on the test print will produce a proper colour balance on the final print.

With experience, you will probably be able to judge filtration by eye as accurately without the calculator as with it.

VIEWING AIDS

Because correct filtration is so essential to colour printing, various aids are available which make it easier for you to learn filtration and in general speed the process of making adjustments when needed.

The aids presented below can be useful, but be careful not to rely on them so much that they become crutches instead of aids. There is no substitute for your own knowledge.

VIEWING FILTERS

The Kodak Colour Print Viewing Filter Kit can be extremely useful in helping you learn to analyse prints and make filter corrections. To use the kit, you simply find the card and "window" (see photograph below) through which the colours in a test print appear in correct balance. A notation below the window then tells you the correction to make in your enlarger's filter pack. Read one side of the card if you are printing from transparencies and the other side if you are printing from negatives.

CC and CP filters

The most basic aids are the same colour-compensating or colour-printing filters you use in your enlarger. (Of course, you may not own these filters if your enlarger has a dichroic head.) First, analyse the print by eye to decide which colour is out of balance. Next, regardless of whether you are printing from a transparency or a negative, consult the chart on p. 109 and view the print through the recommended filter or filters. Make any further adjustments until the colours in the print look correct to your eye. (Be sure to view both the original and the print in the same light.) Finally, if you are printing from a slide, simply add the correcting filters to the enlarger's filter pack, remove any neutral density, and expose your print. If you are printing from a negative, you must *subtract* the correction from the enlarger's filter pack (or consult the chart on p. 110 to find the proper filters to *add* to the filter pack, if subtraction is not possible).

Using CC and CP filters in this way works, but is inconvenient and can be confusing, especially when printing from negatives. Viewing filters (described at left) are a more convenient alternative.

Colour calculators

Colour calculators function on the principle that if a photograph that contains all colours is properly filtered and exposed, scrambling the colours should produce a neutral grey tone. Colour calculators contain a diffusion filter that you place over your enlarger lens to blend together the colours in a transparency or negative, and a perforated card that you lay upon your printing paper before you make the exposure. The scrambled light passes through holes in the card which contain a wide range of filter combinations and densities. Once you have processed and dried the print, you compare the coloured discs formed on the print by the filters to a standard grey which has been printed on the type of paper you are using. The disc that matches the standard grey signals the adjustments required in your filter pack to achieve proper colour balance. In addition, a separate series of discs indicates exposure corrections.

Test prints made using a colour calculator can be hard to "read" if the print requires only minor filtration corrections, but for correcting gross filtration errors, such as those which occur when changing to a new paper batch, a colour calculator can be useful.

Colour analysers

Once you have determined the correct filtration to use with a particular paper batch, a colour analyser enables you to make subsequent prints from different slides or negatives without needing to make additional test prints. If you regularly print from properly exposed transparencies onto one basic paper type, you probably will not need to make enough test prints to justify the relatively high initial cost of a colour analyser.

A colour analyser works by electronically comparing the colours in a negative to a "standard" negative for which you have already determined the correct filtration. As long as you do not change to a different paper batch or switch to a different processing chemistry, the analyser will tell you very precisely how to change the enlarger's filter pack so that a new slide or negative will produce a print with colours in the same balance as the standard you used to programme the analyser.

You will obtain the best results if your standard negative contains tones you can readily identify from photograph to photograph – flesh tones and neutral greys work especially well – and if it is shot under the same conditions (e.g. outdoors, indoors, etc.) as the photographs to which it will be compared.

When you change to a different paper, you must programme the analyser again to your standard negative. However, if you maintain a record of the enlarger filter packs and analyser settings that correspond to each paper and emulsion batch you use, you will be able to switch from one paper to another with ease.

Although the primary function of colour analysers is to provide filtration information, they have other uses as well.

Exposure control

With either colour or black and white film, you can use the analyser to measure exposure settings.

Contrast grades of paper

You can use the analyser to determine the exposure range in a black and white negative and select a contrast grade of paper that will accommodate that range.

Unusual lighting situation

An analyser can correct for colour imbalances induced by a non-standard light source. (For example, if you shoot tungsten film outdoors, or outdoor film under fluorescent lights, the analyser can auto-

OMEGA SCA-100 COLOR ANALYZER

Reference arrows for cosine alignment

Colour-reading aperture

Cosine correction control aligns the analyzer to the optical center of the enlarger lens

Colour channel selector switch for choosing the colour to be read

Meter filtration and exposure readout scale

Electrostop control and scale adjusts the sensitivity of the individual colours to match the light level of the enlarger

Colour program reference scales for setting the particular colour calibration amount

Colour program dials for cyan, magenta and yellow

matically make corrections when you prepare a print).

Colour analysers may be a luxury, but a luxury worth considering if you need highly accurate filter corrections or if for any reason you find yourself wasting substantial quantities of paper making routine test prints.

A neat colour analyser which swings under the lens of the enlarger and combines with an exposure meter on the baseboard to give accurate colour and exposures.

THE PROCESSING DRUM

Cap with light-trap opening for pouring chemicals in and out

Light-proof drum

Guide rail for motor base

Bottom cap, removable for cleaning

Changeable program timer for stopping and starting the motor base and for signaling the end of each step.

Motor On/Off switch

Motor base

HOW DRUMS WORK

The procedure for loading a drum is to insert, in darkness, a sheet of exposed printing paper, emulsion side facing in (i.e. away from the drum wall); cap the drum ends; then, in room light, pour about $2\frac{1}{2}$ oz (70 ml) of chemicals into a reservoir in one of the end caps. Once you lay the drum on its side, the chemicals spill onto the print and timing begins. When the processing time expires, drain the chemicals via the same opening through which they were introduced, or, in some cases, through an opening in the opposite end of the drum.

DIFFERENT SIZES OF DRUMS

Processing drums come in a variety of makes and sizes which correspond to standard paper sizes. By choosing the correct size for the paper you are using, you will use smaller quantities of chemicals. The large drum at right can hold one 20"x24" (51x61 cm) print, two 16"x20" (41x51 cm) prints, or six 8"x10" prints, using in each instance the same 8 oz (228 ml) of chemistry.

Processing drums are hollow, light-tight plastic cylinders in which you process exposed printing paper. A special opening in one end of the cylinder permits you to pour in and drain out chemicals without admitting light. Internally, some drums are smooth-walled to facilitate cleaning, while others contain grooves to promote circulation of chemicals over the surfaces of the printing paper. Different sizes of drums accommodate a variety of paper sizes, with 8″ x 10″, 11″ x 14″, 16″ x 20″, and 20″ x 24″ (51 x 61 cm) most readily available. Some drums are sold with inserts to make it possible to fit small paper sizes into larger drums.

Advantages

Drum processing requires less bench space than dish processing; it can be performed with the room lights on; and it uses chemicals far more economically than dishes do.

Disadvantages

A single 8″ x 10″ drum is somewhat more expensive than the dishes you would need to perform the same process. Also, many types of drums can accommodate only a single sheet of printing paper at a time.

What to buy

You will need at least one drum to handle the size of paper you expect to use most frequently. If you also want the ability to print on smaller paper, choose a model with special inserts for the purpose. If you

plan to make many 8″ x 10″ prints, you may want to consider a 20″ x 24″ drum which can accommodate six 8″ x 10″ prints at once. Even if you make prints predominantly of one size, you may still want to purchase an assortment of drums in order to process more than one size at a time and in order to avoid wasting chemicals (as happens when a small print is processed in a large drum). If the processes you expect to use more frequently require high temperatures, you may want to select a model with watertight ends so the drum can be immersed in a temperature-controlled water bath.

Agitation

In order to agitate by hand, you repeatedly roll the drum one complete revolution back and forth across a flat surface. *Motorized agitator bases* produce a much smoother agitation than is possible by hand. Some bases rotate the drum in only one direction, but the better bases turn first in one direction, then the other. The very best bases also produce a rocking motion which prevents streaks by ensuring uniform chemical distribution across the entire surface of the paper. Some processes require manual agitation at high speed for a few seconds before the drum can be placed on the slower, motorized base.

Replenishment

Since only about 2½ oz (70 ml) of chemistry are used in a drum with most processes, most chemicals are completely depleted after one use and must be discarded.

RIBS INSIDE DRUM
This drum has adjustable ribs so that it can be made to accommodate various paper sizes. The clips on the rib at the top of the drum are used to keep odd-size prints in place.

HOW TO USE THE DRUM

Load the drum so that the emulsion side of the paper faces the drum's centre. If the drum you are using contains adjustable ribs to accommodate different paper sizes, be sure the paper fits between the ribs securely.

Pre-measure the correct amount of chemistry for the paper size you are using, then pour the liquid rapidly into the drum's opening. Begin agitating immediately so that the chemistry does not "pool" on one section of the print. (The particular drum shown above is designed so that "pooling" cannot occur.)

Drain the contents of the drum quickly, making certain no residual liquid remains to dilute the next chemical.

When using a drum you can obtain excellent results with minimum difficulty, as long as you observe some basic rules carefully. A complete trial run-through using water instead of chemicals will familiarize you with procedures in a non-critical atmosphere. Once you begin processing a real print, you cannot stop to read directions without ruining your print.

CLEANLINESS

Chemicals are easily contaminated. To keep pure the chemicals that come in contact with your prints, wash your processing drum thoroughly with warm or hot water after each use, and then dry the drum completely. Careful drying will prevent droplets of water from streaking a print between the time the paper is loaded and the time agitation begins.

LOADING

The emulsion side of the printing paper must always face the centre of the drum, *not* the drum wall. If you are loading more than one print in a drum, be especially careful not to let the prints overlap, or

else areas of incomplete development will result. After loading the drum, be certain that its end caps are on tightly enough to prevent light leakage. On drums that use pins and grooves to guide alignment of the end caps, make sure the pins are properly engaged in the grooves.

AGITATION

If you are agitating manually, roll the drum back and forth with a constant, steady motion as in the photograph sequence at right. Do not let the drum stop rolling for longer than an instant when changing direction, or your print will show the effects of uneven development. Start timing as soon as the drum begins its first roll, and continue steady agitation until it is time to start pouring out the drum's contents.

PROCESSING COLOUR PRINTS IN DISHES

You can process more than one print at a time in a dish of colour chemistry; however, during each processing step you will have to move the bottom print to the top every few seconds to ensure that each print continually receives fresh chemistry and proper agitation. Since you must perform this exchange procedure in total darkness, you will have to set up each dish beforehand or the process will not flow smoothly. Be sure to wear rubber gloves to protect your hands, and be careful when handling prints not to damage the emulsions, which are soft when wet and easily scratched or torn.

COLOUR PRINTS FROM NEGATIVES
Kodak Ektaprint 2

Kodak Ektaprint 2 processing kit

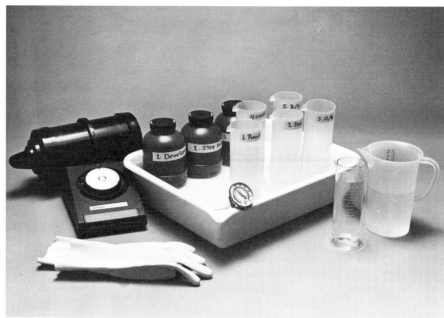

SET-UP FOR KODAK EKTAPRINT 2
1. **Processing drum.**
2. **Timer.**
3. **Rubber gloves.**
3. **Chemistry in a temperature-controlled water bath.**
4. **Containers of hot and cold water for controlling the water-bath temperature.**

Use. Kodak Ektaprint 2 chemistry is used for processing Kodak Ektacolor 78 RC and Photocolor RC papers.

Capacities. 1 gallon size. 1 quart (.94 l) develops twelve 8″ x 10″ prints.

Shelf life. Once mixed, 6–8 weeks in full, stoppered bottles.

Processing temperatures. You will obtain the highest quality prints possible if you process at 32.8 ± 0.33°C (91 ± ½°F), but by increasing developing and bleach-fixing times, you can process at temperatures as low as 20°C (68°F).

Processing times. Total processing time requires 7½ minutes at 32.8°C (91°F) and 27 minutes at 20°C (68°F).

Depletion compensation. Ektaprint 2 chemicals should be discarded after one use.

Presoaking. For drum processing there is an additional presoak step to prevent the developer from causing streaks on the paper.

Mixing chemicals. Because of the presoak step, chemical concentrations for drum processing must be stronger than for dish processing. Be sure to follow the mixing instructions for "tube processing" packed with the chemicals. You can make your own stop bath solution by adding 48 ml of 28% acetic acid to 1 litre of water. (To make 28% acetic acid, add three parts of glacial acetic acid to eight parts water.) *Caution:* Always add acid to water, not water to acid.

Advantages. Ektaprint 2 chemicals are specifically designed for use with Kodak papers and will yield high quality results with Photocolor and some Agfa papers as well.

PROCESSING SUMMARY FOR EKTAPRINT 2

Step	Temp. °C	Temp. °F	Time (min.)	Amt. of Soln. for 8″ x 10″ print ml.	Amt. of Soln. for 8″ x 10″ print ozs.
1. Presoak	33	91	½	500*	17.5
2. Develop	33	91	3½*	70	2.5
3. Stop Bath	33	91	½	50	1.75
4. Bleach-Fix	33	91	1*	50	1.75
5. Wash	33	91	2**	500	17.5
6. Dry	not over 107°	225°			
Total Time			8 minutes		

*If the drum does not hold 500 ml (17.5 ozs), then fill to capacity.

**Transfer print to a dish, then drain and fill four times, agitating 30 seconds each time for 2 minutes.

There are many ingenious designs of paper processors and this orbital model with a whirling action is one of the latest. It is economical to buy and does not take much solution. The pre-soak chart lying on top is seen in more detail on page 127.

COLOUR PRINTS FROM COLOUR NEGATIVES AND COLOUR TRANSPARENCIES
Kodak Ektaflex

The Ektaflex Printer showing the guides for the negative and the paper as well as the handle by which the sandwich is wound out. Once out, the room light can be turned on.

This very much simplified process for making colour prints from colour negatives or transparencies was introduced by Kodak in 1982. It is based on the image-transfer process used in Kodak Instant colour film, and it employs a single activator solution in conjunction with a compact print-making machine. The cost of the printmaker is under £100 and the outlay should prove well worthwhile for any amateur who makes a regular practice of colour printing at home. At present it is limited to a maximum size of 8″ x 10″ prints.

The negative or transparency is placed in the enlarger holder emulsion side up because the image is transferred in processing. The starting points for exposure times, filtration and lens aperture are given with the materials. Exposure is made by suitable safelight or preferably in the dark, onto Ektaflex PCT Negative film when working from colour negatives, and PCT Reversal film when employing colour transparencies. The film is code-notched to ensure that it is placed emulsion side up. A sheet of Ektaflex PCT Paper is placed on the paper shelf of the printmaker emulsion side down and the exposed film is placed emulsion side up on to the film loading ramp of the printmaker. It is then slid smoothly into the Activator solution in the machine where it soaks for 20 seconds. The film sheet is laminated to the paper 5 seconds before the soak time is up by turning the handle at the side, and this is continued until the sandwich emerges. After 6 to 15 minutes, according to room temperature, they can be peeled apart. No washing is required and the print is damp-dry. It can be dried off very quickly with warm air from a print drier and, of course, new prints can be made while others are being activated.

It is possible to experiment with solarisation and other creative effects by making a second print from the same sheet of film, being careful to ensure that multiple printing is not more than one or two seconds in order that there is no risk of contamination of the activator solution.

Since the developers and process control layers have been incorporated in the products the need for bleaching, fixing, stabilization, agitation and temperature control has been eliminated. The colour reproduction is excellent and comparable with that produced by conventional Ektacolor and Ektachrome papers. At present the process works out at a little higher cost per print but, apart from the cost of the Printmaker, it is very much simpler and more time saving, so the cost is likely to come down in due course. Likewise, we may well see machines and materials for larger sizes in the not too distant future.

Ektaflex PCT Activator

Available in 2,84 litre pack which processes approximately 75 prints 8" x 10" (20.3 x 25.4 cm). It is effective in temperatures from 18°C to 26.5°C (65°F to 80°F). Its active life in the dish is about 72 hours, but if returned to the container and properly sealed it will last up to 12 months.

Ektaflex PCT Negative Film

For making colour prints from colour negatives. Available in 10 and 25 sheet packs and 5" x 7" (12.7 x 17.8 cm) or 8" x 10" (20.3 x 25.7 cm) sizes. The 8" x 10" sheets are also available in packs of 100. Negative film should be refrigerated when not in use.

Ektaflex PCT Reversal Film

For making prints from transparencies. Available in the same sizes and packs as the negative film. It should also be refrigerated.

Ektaflex PCT Paper

Available with F (smooth glossy) and N (smooth semi-matt) surfaces. Sizes are $5\frac{1}{8}$" x $7\frac{1}{4}$" (13 x 18.4 cm) and $8\frac{1}{8}$" x $10\frac{1}{4}$" (20.6 x 26 cm) and in 10 sheet and 25 sheet packs, plus 100 sheet packs for the larger sizes only.

No refrigeration is required and they should be stored in the original package.

COLOUR PRINTS FROM TRANSPARENCIES
Kodak Ektaprint R14-3

Kodak Ektaprint R14 processing kit

SET-UP FOR KODAK EKTAPRINT R14
1. **Processing drum.**
2. **Timer.**
3. **Rubber gloves.**
4. **Chemistry in a temperature-controlled water bath.**
5. **Containers of hot and cold water for controlling the water-bath temperature.**

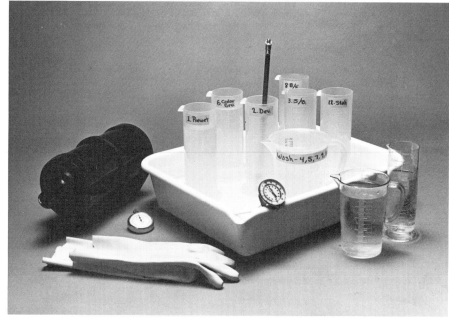

KODAK R14-3

Use. Kodak R14 chemistry is used for processing Ektachrome RC 14 paper for prints made directly from colour transparencies (slides).

Capacity. 1 quart develops 13 8" x 10" prints.

Shelf life. After mixing, 4–8 weeks in full, stoppered bottles, 2–4 weeks in partially filled bottles.

Processing temperature. 38°C (100°F). The starting temperature of chemicals can be raised to produce an average processing temperature of 38°C (100°F), but a constant-temperature water bath gives the best results.

Processing time. $13\frac{1}{4}$ minutes.

Depletion compensation. R14 chemicals should be discarded after one use.

Presoaking. For drum processing there is an additional presoak step to prevent the developer from causing streaks on the paper.

Kodak RC14 paper. The paper used with R14 processing requires careful handling. Exposure must take place in total darkness because the paper is sensitive to all wavelengths of light. If you have no basis for selecting a beginning filtration, try 20 Cyan and 20 Magenta if your

transparency was taken on Kodachrome, 30 Cyan and 20 Magenta for Ektachrome. Due to the potential effects of reciprocity failure, if at all possible keep exposure time to 10 seconds or less. Processing should take place no more than 8 hours after exposure.

Alternative processing temperatures and times. Instructions packaged with R14 chemicals provide information on processing at temperatures as low as 21°C (70°F). At the lower temperatures, processing time must be increased; at 21°C (70°F), the total processing time becomes $31\frac{1}{4}$ minutes instead of $13\frac{1}{4}$ minutes.

R14-3 processing steps. If you have processed colour prints previously, the information summarized in the chart on the next page will be sufficient for you to successfully process a colour print using R14 chemicals. If you have never before processed a colour print, study the step by step instructions for the Cibachrome process in the next section. R14 and Cibachrome differ in specifics, but not in skills required. Once you think you understand how each step in colour processing is performed, verify your understanding by making a trial run following R14 instructions but without using paper, and using plain water instead of chemicals.

Kodak Ektaprint R14-3

Steps for tube processing of Kodak Ektachrome RC14 paper using Kodak Ektaprint R14 chemicals.

Step	Temperature °C	°F	Time* min.	Amount of solution per 8″ x 10″ print
1. Presoak	38	100	1	150 ml (5 oz)
2. First Developer	38	100	2	70 ml (2.5 oz)
3. Stop Bath	38	100	$\frac{1}{2}$	70 ml (2.5 oz)
4. Wash	38	100	1	150 ml (5 oz)
5. Wash	38	100	1	150 ml (5 oz)
6. Colour Developer	38	100	2	70 ml (2.5 oz)
7. Wash	38	100	$\frac{1}{2}$	150 ml (5 oz)
8. Bleach/Fix	38	100	3	70 ml (2.5 oz)
9. Wash	38	100	$\frac{1}{2}$	150 ml (5 oz)
10. Wash	38	100	$\frac{1}{2}$	150 ml (5 oz)
11. Wash	38	100	$\frac{1}{2}$	150 ml (5 oz)
12. Stabilizer	38	100	$\frac{1}{2}$	70 ml (2.5 oz)
13. Rinse (Water)	38	100	$\frac{1}{4}$	150 ml (5 oz)

*These times include a 10 second drain time or the drain time you have determined for your tube processor.

A pre-soak temperature calculator by which precise control can be exercised. The reverse side gives temperatures in Fahrenheit.

COLOUR PRINTS FROM TRANSPARENCIES
Cibachrome A-II

Processing a colour print requires that you combine elements of preparation, organization, precision, and attention to detail if you are to achieve quality results with consistency. Different processes call for different procedures, but there are enough similarities among the processes that, if you can perform one process with proficiency, you will easily be able to transfer the skills from that process to another.

In this section, the Cibachrome process for making prints from transparencies is described in detail, step by step. The Cibachrome process has been chosen as an example for a variety of reasons: it is unlike other processes, produces very high quality prints, involves only three chemicals, has a wide tolerance for temperature deviations, and is simple to execute properly. In short, it is an excellent process to learn if you have never before printed in colour.

Moreover, Ilford markets a Discovery Kit that includes processing chemistry, 4" x 5" paper, and a 4" x 5" processing drum. If you decide after purchasing a Discovery Kit that you do not want to continue processing in colour, you will not have invested an unreasonable amount of money in chemicals and equipment, and if you find that you want to pursue colour processing beyond your first experience, the 4" x 5" drum will always be useful for making test prints.

Two additional washing steps are included in the step by step instructions. They take little extra time but are well worth the effort. Once you can obtain good results consistently, you may try eliminating the extra washes to see if your results are affected.

Use. Cibachrome chemistry must be used for processing prints made from transparencies on Cibachrome A-II paper.

Capacity. 900 ml develops ten 8" x 10" prints.

Shelf life. After mixing: developer, 3 weeks; bleach, 5 weeks; fixer, 1 year.

Processing temperatures. 20–28°C (68–82°F). Recommended: 24 $\pm$ 1½°C (75 $\pm$ 3°F).

Processing times. 10½ minutes at 28°C (82°F); 12 minutes at 24°C (75°F); 14 minutes at 20°C (68°F).

Depletion compensation. Cibachrome chemicals should normally be discarded after one use but partial re-use is possible.

Presoaking. None required.

Mixing chemicals. You can mix Cibachrome chemistry in quantities sufficient for a single 8" x 10" print, for ten 8" x 10" prints, or for twenty 8" x 10" prints. Bleach and fixer can be mixed in 1-quart (900 ml) and ½-gallon (1.9 l) quantities.

Advantages. Cibachrome prints produce sharp images with deep colour saturation. Processing time is moderate, and tolerance of temperature variations during processing ($\pm$ 1½°C, $\pm$ 3°F) is excellent.

Cibachrome paper. Unlike Kodak papers, Cibachrome paper contains colour dyes, which is why black and white developers such as Kodak D23 will work on it. Cibachrome paper is subject to reciprocity failure in exposures longer than 10 seconds, so it is especially important to maintain a standard exposure time and adjust exposure by means of lens aperture. If necessary, exposed paper can be held for a few days before processing. Because the paper's emulsion layers are extremely soft and easily damaged when wet, handle wet prints with extreme care. Also, keep in mind that wet prints have a reddish cast until completely dry. Note that Cibachrome paper must be exposed in total darkness.

Draining. As with most processes, the final drain time in the Cibachrome procedure is included in the agitation time. Determine the particular drain time for your drum, then start pouring out its contents that many seconds before the designated agitation time expires. (10–15 seconds drain time is typical. 10 seconds is used here for illustration purposes.) To avoid contamination or dilution of subsequent chemicals, be certain to allow sufficient time to drain the drum thoroughly.

Disadvantages. Cibachrome prints cost more to produce than Kodak prints. Also, some people criticise Cibachrome prints for having too much contrast, but in most prints the increased contrast is not noticeable. In the cases where contrast is a problem, it can be reduced by either shortening development time by 30 seconds or switching to a "softer" developer such as Kodak D23 and then experimenting to find the best development time and filtration.

Temperature. If the temperature at which you are processing exceeds room temperature, you will need to place all chemicals and wash waters in a temperature-adjusted water bath. In addition, you must control the temperature of chemicals within the processing drum. If your drum is watertight, you can maintain temperature by performing the agitation steps in a water bath. Otherwise, you will have to make certain the *average* temperature of the chemicals in the drum equals the recommended temperature. You can do this by starting with chemicals a few degrees too *warm* so that when the agitation time is over, their temperature will have become a few degrees too *cool*. You can experiment with 2–3 oz of water in an empty drum to find the best starting temperature.

Organization. Regardless of the process you choose, the care with which you organize your materials can affect the quality of your results. Before you begin, make certain all equipment is at hand and all chemicals are at the proper temperature. Place your chemical bottles in the order you will need them, and have sufficient water ready for the washes required by the process. Have a bag of ice or a supply of hot water nearby if you will need to control processing temperatures precisely. And do not forget to wear rubber gloves to prevent chemical burns.

Cibachrome A-II

Step	Temperature	Time
1. Developer	24°C (75°F)	3 min.
2. Rinse	24°C (75°F)	30 sec.
3. Bleach*	24°C (75°F)	3 min.
4. Rinse	$24 \pm 1°C$ ($75 \pm 3°F$)	30 sec.
5. Fixer	$24 \pm 1°C$ ($75 \pm 3°F$)	3 min.
6. Wash**	20 to 24°C (68 to 75°F)	3 min.

 * Neutralize used bleach in a bucket, as per the manufacturer's instructions.

** The print is carefully removed from the drum and washed under running water in a dish. Do not wash the print in the drum.

Note: Steps 2 and 4 can be omitted if desired but not recommended.

CIBACHROME A-II
Step by step

CIBACHROME, STEP BY STEP

Detailed instructions for processing Ciba-chrome colour printing paper are illus-trated on this and the following three pages. Be sure to read pp. 128-129 before starting. Many of the procedures shown here (for example, agitation) are applic-able to drum processing in general, regardless of the specific chemistry being used.

CIBACHROME

1. *Load paper in drum,* emulsion side *in.*
2. *Cap drum ends.*
3. *Turn on lights.*

4. *Pour neutralizer powder into waste bucket.* This step is omitted with Cibachrome AII.

5. *Check temperature of chemicals.* Place in a water bath, if necessary.

6. *Set timer* for 2 minutes.

7. *Pour developer into drum.*
8. *Start agitation. Start timer.*

9. *Agitate* one complete back-and-forth revolution per second for 15 seconds (must be done manually even if a motorized base is available).
10. *Agitate continuously thereafter* on a motorized base, or manually at the rate of 40 complete back-and-forth revolutions pers minute.

11. *Drain drum,* pouring out the developer *starting 10 seconds* before the developing time expires.

12. *Pour wash water into drum.*
13. *Agitate* for 10 seconds.

14. *Drain drum thoroughly.*

15. *Set timer* for 4 minutes.

16. *Pour bleach into drum.*

CIBACHROME A-II (Continued)
Step by step

17. *Start agitation. Start timer.*
18. *Agitate* one complete back-and-forth revolution per second for 15 seconds (must be done manually even if a motorized base is available).
19. *Agitate continuously thereafter* on a motorized base, or manually at the rate of 40 back-and-forth revolutions per minute.

20. *Drain drum* into a bucket containing the neutralizer, starting 10 seconds before the bleaching time expires. Neutralizer is not necessary with the improved AII process.

21. *Pour wash water into drum.*
22. *Agitate* for 10 seconds.

23. *Drain drum thoroughly.*

24. *Set timer* for 3 minutes.

25. *Pour fixer into drum.*

26. *Start agitation. Start timer.*

27. *Agitate continuously* on a motorized base or manually at the rate of 40 back-and-forth revolutions per minute.
28. *Drain drum,* pouring out the fixer starting 10 seconds before the developing time expires.

29. *Remove print from drum.*

30. *Wash print in tray* for at least 3 minutes in running water.
31. *Remove print from tray.*

32. *Place print on towel* or another soft, absorbent surface.
33. *Squeegee front and back surfaces* (optional)

34. *Dry prints* using by either drying rack, hanging them, or blowing them with a hair dryer.

7. SPECIAL TECHNIQUES

This photograph was made from a 35 mm negative that was reticulated during processing and then, after processing, was frozen while still wet. Manipulative procedures such as this should be tried only on copy negatives, since the results are both unpredictable and permanent.

As we have already stressed, your first priority should be to master the fundamentals of darkroom processing until they become second nature to you. However, after you have confidence in your mastery of the basics, you may want to try your hand at some of the advanced techniques of printing, and thereby experience what many photographers consider to be the chief attractions and benefits of do-it-yourself processing.

Many of the techniques described in this chapter involve substantial alteration to create the way an image ultimately appears. Although it is true that what looks horrible to one person may seem perfectly acceptable to another, it is also true that few things are more jarring than a photograph on which an inappropriate manipulative technique has been used. Therefore, to avoid wasting your time and money on results that might appear gimmicky, you should employ a specific technique only when you have a clear aesthetic reason for using it, and you know what the effect will be in advance. By having a clearly defined *aesthetic intent* when you use a special technique, its effects are more likely to appear in harmony with the original image.

Some of the techniques described here involve altering the original negative or slide. In order to prevent alterations from becoming permanent, you may want to perform them on *duplicate* negatives and slides, as explained on the following pages. By making duplicates you will always have an intact original image to which you can return if, despite your careful planning, something goes awry, or if you find that the effect you have produced is not as pleasing as you had anticipated. If you exercise care in making the duplicates, their quality will be only slightly diminished from that of the originals. In addition, the very process of duplication introduces opportunities for manipulation which can be effective in their own right.

COPYING EQUIPMENT

Camera body
with right-angle finder
mounted on the bellows

Magnification scale

Partially reflective glass
to pass pure light
through the lens

Light output
for contrast control

Flash sync cord

Slide holder

Light measurement scale

Light meter

**Light-meter
readout scale**

On–off switch

**Focusing-light
on–off switch**

**Contrast-control
cable**

Open-flash switch

**Light-intensity
adjustment knob**

**Flash-intensity
control switch**

"Trimmer"
for fine tuning
meter scale

THE BOWENS ILLUMITRAN
The Bowens Illumitran is one of the
sophisticated devices available for copying
slides by flash illumination. The Illumitran
incorporates an ingenious device that helps
to lower contrast by controlled fogging from a
second flash.

duced by using lens-extension tubes, a bellows extender, or a macro lens. (Supplementary close-up lenses, which attach like a filter, introduce too much distortion.

Home made systems

As long as you use a camera and lens of good quality and take care to align all elements precisely, you will be able to make excellent copies with an improvised home made system. The most basic arrangement consists of a tripod-mounted camera fitted with a bellows extender or macro lens that is capable of delivering a subject-image enlargement ratio of at least 1:1. In such a system, you place the transparency or negative to be copied on a sheet of white cardboard which is placed below the camera. If you expect to make many copies, you can build a more permanent device by constructing a small wooden box with a frosted acetate top, such as the one shown at right. In one side of the box, cut an opening in which a flash unit will fit; then mount a piece of white cardboard inside the box at a 45° angle so that the cardboard reflects the light coming through the opening up towards the top of the box. Finally, install a small tungsten lamp inside the box to provide enough light for focusing. You will need to ascertain the best exposure by experiment, but once determined, the exposure usually remains relatively constant. If you want to, you can place filters under the transparency or negative being copied to adjust colour or produce special effects.

A *high-quality* image can be produced by using an enlarger lens, since the way enlarger lenses are designed minimizes image distortion when used for close-up photography. "Normal" lenses, that is, lenses with a focal length approximately equal to the diagonal of the film size (50 mm with 35 mm film) can also be used. If you use a normal lens, it should be reversed by means of a reversing ring when the distance between the item being copied and the front of the lens is less than the distance between the rear of the lens and the film.

There are several makes of self-contained units consisting of a tube with

To make high-quality copies you need three elements: a source of even illumination, a method of producing an image on film at least as large as the transparencies or negatives being duplicated, and a lens which will not produce distortion at magnifications of 1:1 or greater.

The *light source* can be daylight, a tungsten lamp, or an electronic flash unit. The light can be made even by reflecting it off a white surface or by passing it through frosted acetate or glass.

Sufficient *magnification* can be pro-

AUXILIARY COPYING DEVICE
Although copying devices like the one at right are inexpensive to buy and easy to use with either daylight or tungsten illumination, the optics these devices contain are usually inferior to a regular camera or enlarger lens used on a bellows.

its own optical elements, which you mount on your camera in place of a standard lens. You place your transparency or negative in one end of the tube and any desired colour-correction or special effects filters in the other. (Some models permit cropping.) If your camera has through-the-lens metering, and you use daylight or tungsten illumination, exposure determinations are simple. Otherwise, you must experiment or bracket your shots to be certain to achieve a correct exposure.

Bowens Illumitran

One of the advanced devices available for duplicating is the Illumitran made by Bowens. This piece of equipment contains its own built-in flash system and employs a very sophisticated method for controlling copy contrast (p. 134). The Illumitran is fitted with a bellows extender to allow great cropping versatility, and a filter drawer to make colour correction and special effects possible. However, you must add your own camera body and lens to the basic unit.

Omega copy attachment

For use with its dichroic enlarger head, Omega makes an attachment that allows you to mount a camera body where the enlarger head usually sits and thereby convert the head into a copying light source (see photograph). Because the head contains built-in dichroic filters, colour correction is simple. Moreover, cropping is easy. If you already own an Omega enlarger, this attachment provides you with an inexpensive means for producing excellent duplicates.

**OMEGA TRANSPARENCY-COPY
ENLARGER ATTACHMENT**
A simple accessory manufactured by Omega converts their C-700 dichroic enlarger head into a convenient, colour-correcting transparency copier.

To use the attachment, you remove the enlarger head, lay it upside down on the enlarger baseboard, and install the accessory where the head usually sits. The accessory then permits you to mount your camera body, as shown above, and photograph a negative or transparency placed on the enlarger head. This set-up produces excellent results when used with Kodak 35mm Ektachrome Duplicating Film.

HOME-MADE TRANSPARENCY COPIER
You can construct your own slide copier by mounting a flash, a viewing bulb, and a white reflective surface inside a box. The opening for the transparency should be covered with a small square of frosted acrylic pastic.

MAKING COPIES

SLIDE SANDWICH
The photograph of a plane flying across the sun is actually a black and white copy of a "sandwich" made from the two transparencies opposite. The two transparencies were removed from their mounts, cleaned thoroughly, mounted together, and copied onto Kodachrome film using the Bowens Illumitran. The image of the plane was so dark when placed over the sun photograph that a compensation of three *f*-stops was needed to achieve an acceptable exposure.

Each time you make a copy you will find that the dark tones become darker and the light tones become lighter. For the most part, the usefulness of a film or item of equipment for copying relates directly to its ability to minimize the increase in contrast, or to compensate for it. Another potential problem is an unwanted increase in film grain size. Recently, colour duplicating films have been improved to the point where they produce only extremely small increases in contrast and no noticeable increase in grain size. Duplicating films are sold in 35mm rolls (designated Ektachrome 5071 for tungsten light and SO-366 for flash) and in sheets (designated Ektachrome 6121).

If your light source is sunlight or a flash, you have little choice other than to use Kodachrome 25 if you want to obtain as exact a duplicate as possible. The grain of Kodachrome 25 has such excellent resolution that using it for making copies introduces no grain-related problems, but contrast does become significantly greater. To camouflage the increase in contrast, Kodachrome 25 can be "flashed" with a burst of white light. The flash, which must be carefully controlled to prevent the entire frame from becoming over-exposed, compensates for the additional contrast by lightening the dark tones on the film. Flashing does nothing to replace lost detail in the shadow and highlight areas of the image, but it does make dark areas appear lighter. An important attribute of the Bowen's Illumitran is that it contains a device that controls flashing quite accurately.

Another way to control contrast with Kodachrome 25 is to have a special "contrast-control mask" prepared by a commercial laboratory; however, such masks are very expensive.

With black and white film, you can minimize contrast increase by under-developing. The amount to under-develop varies according to the copy technique, but try reducing development time by 20% at first. If contrast remains high, under-develop your next roll of film even more. If your negatives begin to appear too weak, however, you must slightly increase development time again.

COLOUR FILTRATION

Any time you copy a colour transparency or negative onto colour film, you will be faced with colour-filtration considerations similar to those you must face when making colour prints. Specifically, you must use filters to balance the colour of your light source with the characteristics of your batch of film. Since each time you change to a new emulsion batch you must determine another filtration, you should set aside as many rolls of film from a single emulsion batch as you think you will use before the film's expiration date. Then perform a filtration test as follows:

1. Select transparency or negative showing a range of colours and some flesh tones.
2. Determine the filtration to use by consulting the instructions packaged with the film.
3. Place the suggested filter between your light source and the transparency or negative to be copied.
4. Copy the original onto the test film.
5. Process the test film normally.
6. Use the techniques described in Chapter Six to determine which filters you will need to add or subtract to achieve a correct colour balance. (If you are copying a negative onto duplicating film, or a transparency onto negative film, you will need to make a print before you can evaluate the filtration.)

4" x 5" FILM

You can avoid the necessity for special duplicating equipment by enlarging your transparency or negative onto 4" x 5" duplicating film. The technique involves placing the original in your enlarger and projecting it onto the baseboard. After adjusting image size and focusing, you turn off the enlarger lamp, take out a sheet of 4" x 5" duplicating film, place it in the baseboard just as you would a sheet of printing paper, expose the film, and then process it. This technique will provide you with excellent duplicates, but, of course, your enlarger head must be able to accommodate 4" x 5" film if you are to print from the duplicate, and you must have a 4" x 5" sheet-film developing tank if you want to process the film yourself.

EXPOSURE

The same exposure principles that apply to macrophotography apply to transparency and negative copying. Through-the-lens metered cameras make exposure determinations with daylight or tungsten bulbs easy, whereas other types of cameras and light sources require either exposure calculations or a series of test exposures. Once you have determined the best exposure for your particular setup, however, you will find that the exposure remains fairly constant unless you change the enlargement size substantially.

FILM

Because Kodak Ektachrome duplicating film produces an exact positive copy of the original, rather than a negative copy, duplicating in colour requires only a single step. To reproduce black and white negatives requires two steps: a copy and then a copy of the copy in order to obtain another negative, or you can use Agfa Dia-Direct Film for one-step duplicating. Sometimes you may prefer to make a black and white print from the negative, then photograph the print as a means of producing a copy.

SLIDE SANDWICH

Often a dull transparency can be "sandwiched" with another transparency and a duplicate can be made of the combination. The duplicate then becomes the "original" for the purpose of making prints. Because the degree of enlargement required for 35 mm copying results in very shallow depth-of-field, you must remove the mounts from the transparencies involved in the sandwich and place them in contact with each other. Otherwise, the distance between the film surfaces caused by the thickness of the slide mounts may cause one image or the other to be out of focus in the copy.

HIGH CONTRAST PRINTING

PRODUCING HIGH CONTRAST

If an image you have on film has distinct lines that you would like to emphasise, you can eliminate all grey tones from your final print by either transferring the image to special high-contrast films or making a series of contact prints on very thin paper.

High-contrast film

Kodalith Ortho grade 2556, type 3 film, intended for use by graphic artists and printers, is the film most commonly used for producing extremely high contrast. Kodalith film is sold in 100-foot 35mm rolls or in sheet-film sizes. (4″ x 5″ film is easier to work with and retouch than 35mm film, so if your enlarger can accommodate the larger size, by all means use it.)

Kodalith film produces a negative image; therefore, if you are starting from a negative, you will need a second copy step to obtain an image from which you can make a positive print. If you are starting from a transparency, you can use the first-step copy to make a print on negative paper. Also, if the first-step copy does not eliminate all greys, you will need to make additional steps.

Kodalith film is orthochromatic – not sensitive to red light – so you can work with it under a 1A safelight. Be careful when copying colour transparencies onto Kodalith, however, because red areas on the original will appear black on the copy.

Retouching

You can eliminate blemishes and unwanted detail by drawing directly on the duplicating film in one of the copying steps. You can use waterproof ink or a felt-tip pen. Any marks you make will appear white in the next copy.

Choosing an image

Since you will be reducing the original image to pure black and white, try starting with an image that already shows good contrast. Areas of white or light grey will totally disappear, and areas of medium or dark grey will become completely black.

CONVERTING TO HIGH CONTRAST

Three generations of Kodalith copies were needed to transform the barn photograph opposite into the high-contrast image at left. First, the negative was enlarged onto 4″ x 5″ (10 x 13 cm) Kodalith film. Next, after processing and spotting with a felt-tip pen, the positive Kodalith image was contact printed with another sheet of Kodalith film which yielded a new, high-contrast negative. Finally, the second negative was enlarged onto paper to produce the finished photograph.

Note how the very contrasty light in the original scene produced sharp shadows which converted effectively into a line image. The same scene photographed on an overcast day might not produce enough detail in the barn wood or the tall grass to form the basis for a high-contrast print.

Some manipulation in the form of retouching may be necessary to restore lost details.

Developing

You must decide on the development process you are going to use *before* you expose Kodalith film, since your decision determines the film's ASA/ISO speed. You might try using ASA/ISO with processing in Kodalith Developer ($2\frac{3}{4}$ minutes at 20°C (68°F) or ASA/ISO 25 with processing in Kodak D-11 ($2\frac{1}{2}$ minutes at 20°C (68°F). See the processing instructions packaged with the film for more specific details.

Paper contact method

If you place a developed print on top of an unexposed sheet of printing paper and expose the combination to light, you will produce a high-contrast contact print of the original image on the second sheet after it is processed. Since the new image will be a negative of the original image, you must repeat the process to obtain a positive image. Because the light must pass through the paper on which the original is printed, exposure will be relatively long and must be determined by experimentation. You can draw directly on any of the print steps and can add or subtract detail by over- or underexposing the print.

DEVELOPING TIMES FOR KODALITH

Developer	ASA/ISO (Tungsten)	Developing time at 20°C (68°F)	Agitation
Kodalith A + B	8	$2\frac{1}{4}$–$3\frac{1}{4}$ min.	Constant
D-11	25	2–3 min.	Constant

MULTIPLE PRINTING

MULTIPLE PRINTING

Occasionally you may find yourself confronted by a negative or transparency that alone is dull, but which, if printed together with another negative or transparency, would be much more interesting. Although the technique for printing two or more negatives or transparencies onto one sheet of paper is an exacting task, the results are often well worth the effort.

Sandwiching negatives or transparencies

The easiest way to make a multiple print is to sandwich two negatives or two transparencies, one on top of the other, before placing them in the enlarger's negative carrier. Sandwiching will not be successful with any two images chosen at random, however. For example, detail in the light area of one scene will not show up if that area is sandwiched against a black or very dark area in the other scene. The technique works best where one of the components of the sandwich is primarily translucent except for the areas that correspond to the lighter areas of the other component.

Note that often the sandwich requires a longer exposure time than either of the images it contains.

Successive exposures

A more versatile and more difficult method for printing from multiple negatives or transparencies involves printing first from one image and then from another. By carefully blocking light from some sections of the paper while each exposure is being made, many of the limitations inherent in sandwiching can be overcome. Moreover, you can enlarge two or more images to different sizes in successive exposures.

To produce a multiple print by making successive exposures:

1. Place a piece of white drawing paper cut to the same size as your printing paper on your enlarger's baseboard.
2. Compose one of the images on the drawing paper exactly as you want it on the final print.
3. Sketch an outline of the major components of the image on the drawing paper.
4. Mark the position of the enlarger head on the enlarger column so you can return it to the same height later.

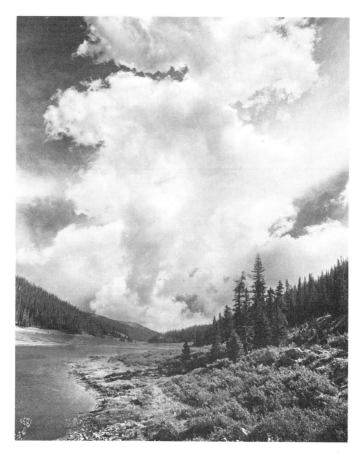

ADDING A DRAMATIC SKY
The inspiring photograph above was made by combining the cloud photograph below with the scenic Rocky Mountain photograph next to it. Since exciting cloud formations are not always available on the spot to perk up an otherwise dull scene, you should collect good sky shots whenever you find them. By doing so you can later add dramatic skies to shots which alone would be lifeless and uninteresting.

142

5. Replace the first negative or transparency with the second.
6. Compose the second image so that it complements the composition of the first image.
7. Sketch an outline of the major components of the second image.
8. Using the sketch as a guide, prepare a mask out of black paper so that while the second image is being exposed, the area where the first image is to be printed will be covered. Then prepare another mask so that while the first image is being exposed, the area containing the second image will be covered.
9. In darkness or under a suitable safe-light, insert a sheet of printing paper in the baseboard.

10. Expose the second image while holding the appropriate mask slightly above the paper and moving it constantly during the exposure (to prevent the edge of the mask from producing a hard line).
11. Transfer the printing paper to a light-tight container. (Make a mental note of how the paper was oriented on the baseboard.)
12. Replace the second negative or transparency with the first, adjust the height of the enlarger head, and compose as before.
13. Return the printing paper to the baseboard.
14. Expose the first image while holding the remaining mask slightly above the paper and moving it constantly during the exposure.
15. Process normally.
(In some instances you will be able to use your hands to cover the necessary areas instead of making paper masks.)

In all likelihood one of your primary goals when processing colour or black and white film will be to produce as sharp an image as possible. Occasionally, however, you may wish to introduce some texture, either by inducing *reticulation* or by using a *texture screen*.

DOUBLE EXPOSURE
With careful preparation and planning, you can use double-exposure techniques to produce unusual – even surrealistic – effects. In the photograph above left, a woman's torso has been superimposed across the sky to echo the outline of the mountains below her. Double exposures are difficult to execute effectively but, when successful, can be quite striking.

A combination print of a nude and a landscape made to give a dramatic presentation which is more evocative than the two pictures on their own.

RETICULATION AND TEXTURE SCREENS

RETICULATED IMAGE
The interesting grain pattern in the above photograph of a woman was achieved by reticulating a copy negative on Panatomic-X, a film not usually recommended for reticulation. The grain pattern is a little finer and more regulated than the pattern that would occur with faster films, but its overall effect enhances the softness suggested by the woman's expression.

RETICULATION

If, instead of maintaining a constant temperature level during the development process, you alternately heat and cool the roll of film, a rhythmic pattern of grainy clumps will form across the surface of the film. These clumps lend the final print a "soft" look that can be quite pleasing. To be safe, you should attempt reticulation only on a duplicate negative, both because the results are somewhat unpredictable and because reticulated emulsions are very soft and therefore easily damaged.

Black and white reticulation
To reticulate black and white film:
1. *Determine development time* for developing at 41°C (105°F) by consulting the film manufacturer's instructions.
2. *Develop film* at 41°C (105°F) for the appropriate time.
3. *Wash in ice water* for 30–60 seconds.
4. *Fix* film as usual at normal temperature in an *acid-hardening* fixer.
5. *Wash film* for 30 minutes in water at normal wash temperature, but do not use a wetting agent.
6. *Hang film* without removing excess water (to avoid damaging the emulsion).
7. *Blow dry* with a hair dryer (optional).

Black and white reticulation, alternative method
The primary drawback to the above technique is the very short development time required by the high development temperature. The following alternative method eliminates that problem.
1. *Develop film* normally, at normal temperature.
2. *Treat with an acetic-acid stop bath* for 60 seconds at 60–66°C (140–150°F).
3. *Wash film* immediately in ice water for 60 seconds.
4. *Fix film* as usual at normal temperature in an *acid-hardening* fixer.
5. *Wash film* for 30 minutes in water at normal wash temperature, but do *not* use a wetting agent.
6. *Hang film* without removing excess water, to avoid damaging emulsion.
7. *Blow dry* with a hair dryer (optional).

For a more dramatic and frostlike reticulation pattern, after processing and while the film is still wet, place it in a freezer for approximately 15 minutes. Also, note that the faster the film you use (the higher its ASA/ISO number), the greater the amount of reticulation that will occur because of thicker emulsions and larger grain structures.

Colour reticulation

Reticulating colour film requires only that you perform a few special steps before following normal processing procedures.
1. *Wash film* for 60 seconds in ice water. *Do not agitate.*
2. *Wash film* in water at the correct processing temperature to raise the film's temperature.
3. *Process film* normally.
4. *Hang film* to dry without removing excess water, to avoid damaging emulsion.

Colour film can be frozen in the same manner as black and white film, but the results vary considerably according to the freezing time (which can be as short as 5 minutes).

TEXTURE SCREENS

While reticulation produces its effect by inducing unpredictable structural changes in a film emulsion, a similar effect can be produced photographically by sandwiching your transparency or negative with a texture screen and copying or printing the two together. One advantage of screens over reticulation is that you can anticipate your results simply by placing the screen over the negative. Texture screens lend themselves equally well to colour and black and white uses.

Commercial screens

You can purchase texture screens in a variety of patterns. Some patterns closely resemble reticulations, some produce an effect reminiscent of film grain, and some imitate fabric textures such as silk, tweed, canvas, or linen.

Improvised screens

You can make your own texture screens without too much difficulty. Start by photographing patterns you like: frost on a window, perhaps, or chipped paint or rippled water. After processing the film, you can either use the frame as it is, or enhance its pattern by copying the image onto high-contrast film to eliminate any distracting grey tones. Sometimes the texture effect will be better if the pattern is sandwiched as a positive instead of as a negative. You will have to experiment.

To make a reticulated texture screen, photograph a neutral grey card and then reticulate the film. Because the reticulated emulsion will be fragile, copy the reticulated negative onto Kodak High Contrast Copy Film. This will also enhance the reticulation effect as well as increase the amount of contrast.

TEXTURE SCREENS
The fabric texture in the photograph below was created by using a texture screen obtained from the kit shown below. Because a 35mm frame is so small, when it is used with a texture screen the texture may appear too prominent. You can minimize the texture effect by copying the 35mm frame onto a larger film size before adding the texture screen and making the final print.

8. DISPLAYING YOUR PHOTOS

Displaying photographs involves much more than simply making them available for viewing. A wide variety of seemingly unimportant factors – the way a photograph is mounted or framed, where it is hung, what surrounds it, and so on – actually has a significant impact on the way a photograph is perceived.

The family pictures shown in the photograph at left were carefully mounted and framed, then all were organized into a coherent grouping. Each photograph tells its own story, and each photograph also contributes to a collective story. Because it was carefully planned and executed, the arrangement not only displays the photographs, it enhances them.

There is little point in spending many hours and much money to take and process photographs if you then banish them to drawers. Outstanding photographs should be seen, appreciated, and even studied. Certainly not every photograph deserves display, but some assuredly do.

The way you display your photographs involves both aesthetic and practical decisions. You want your photographs to look their best, of course, but sometimes your choice of a mounting or framing technique may be dictated by a practical consideration, such as the fact that very large prints often cannot be mounted or framed using methods that work perfectly well with smaller prints. Similarly, if your primary goal is the long-term preservation of a print, you must reject many of the available mounting methods simply because the chemicals involved can help destroy the image.

If you want to show off your photographs to their best advantage even while keeping practical considerations in mind, one approach is to create a consistent style of presentation. For example, a display of a series of your photographs may lend itself well to having all the photographs placed on coloured cardboard mounts and then framed. As you become more and more experienced in preparing such mounts and frames, your technique will become neater and more professional looking. Eventually, you will probably start composing and printing your photographs with your usual mounting or framing technique in mind. The ultimate result of such a consistent use of one perfected method will be photographs that have been executed in a manner appropriate to the way they are mounted or framed – and mounts or frames that are appropriate to the way the photographs have been executed.

No matter how you present your photographs, the amount of care you take in preparing them for display will influence the respect with which they will be regarded. If you mount or frame your photographs thoughtlessly, and with more concern for money saved than aesthetics, then regardless of how good your photographs are, viewers will unconsciously think less of them. Mount or frame your photographs thoughtfully, carefully, and with proper attention to materials – and viewers will accord your work the respect it deserves.

Of course, for every print you decide to mount or frame, there are usually many more you choose not to display, as well as negatives and transparencies you decide not to print. If not discarded, these too must be cared for if they are to last. Store them badly and they will quickly deteriorate; file them haphazardly and you will not be able to find them when you want them. In short, the photographic process is not complete until the fruits of your efforts have been either appropriately displayed or conscientiously stored.

TYPES OF FRAMES AND MOUNTS

FRAME/TYPES
1. **Metal strip frame (unassembled)**
2. **Ready-made wooden strip frame**
3. **Clear plastic box frame**
4. **Ready-made metal strip frame**
5. **Clip frame**

MOUNTS

The term *mount* indicates that a photograph, rather than being framed, is attached to a firm surface, usually by means of an adhesive. "Flush", "box", and "wrap" mountings are all variations on a technique that entails affixing a print onto Masonite or stiff (double-ply) cardboard. All of these methods can be used with prints of any size but are especially effective with larger prints.

Flush mounting

With flush mounting, you trim the edges of your print so that they are even with the edges of the mounting board. You can darken the trimmed white edges of the print with an indelible marker if they are distracting. On the back of the mount you can attach wood strips which will serve both to hold the photograph off the wall and to prevent warping.

Box mounting

With box mounting, you glue wood strips flush with the edges all around the back of a mounted print. The wood strips are usually painted flat black to make them less conspicuous. Box-mounted prints are easy to hang on a wall by means of a single nail.

Wrap mounting

With wrap mounting, you mount your print on a board slightly smaller than the print in order to permit you to wrap and glue the print's edges around the board's edges in a manner similar to wrapping a gift. Wrap mounting must be done very carefully to achieve a neat result.

Murals

Very large prints, mounted by means of one of the above techniques or glued directly onto a wall, are called *murals*. The chief problem murals pose is that any irregularities in the underlying surface or any lumps in the mounting adhesive become very noticeable. Executed with care, however, murals can present a striking appearance.

FRAMES

As mentioned earlier, the care you take in displaying a photograph can either enhance or detract from its effect on a viewer. However, this is not to imply that you must spend a fortune framing every print you make; rather, it suggests that if you decide to frame your photograph, you should exercise good taste and avoid buying a frame that demeans your work simply to save a few pennies. The difference in price between a good frame and a poor one is not really proportionate to the difference in quality. Some of the framing materials from which you can choose are described below.

Clips and corners

Clips and corners are designed to hold together a sandwich composed of a sheet of glass, a mat, a print, and a sheet of stiff cardboard. The clips and corners are small plastic or metal devices connected by strings that run across the back of the assembly from side to side or corner to corner. This method of mounting is inex-

HANGING BORDERLESS PRINTS
Often, borderless prints look best if they are separated from the wall by means of wooden strips to give them the appearance of floating.

TABLE FRAMES
Not every print is best displayed by mounting it on a wall. Small prints especially can be given a feeling of prominence if placed in well-made, carefully chosen table frames.

pensive and in its simplicity does not distract from the print.

Clear plastic frames
One type of inexpensive, ready-made frame consists of a piece of clear plastic moulded in a box configuration with a slightly smaller, white cardboard box fitted inside it. To mount your photograph, you place it on the inside surface of the cardboard, then slip the plastic box over both. Plastic box frames are very simple to use but can look cheap unless intentionally selected for their minimal interference with the appearance of the print itself.

Ready-made frames
Many stores sell simple, already assembled frames in standard sizes such as 5"x7" (13x18 cm), 11"x14" (28x26 cm), and 14"x18" (36x41 cm). Most of the frames consist of a border of gold or silver strips plus a sheet of glass or clear plastic and a mechanism to hold the photograph in place. Frames of this type can be beautiful in their simplicity or startling in their unattractiveness, depending on how well they are made. To avoid shoddy frames, make your purchases at a reputable framing shop or art supply store, rather than a supermarket.

Custom frames
Frames you assemble yourself are similar to the ready-made frames described above, but are sold in 1" size

increments. Assembly is a bit troublesome but not difficult. The primary advantage of using self-assembled, custom frames is that it permits you to construct a frame to fit your print, instead of forcing you to crop your print to fit the frame. In addition, the pieces of the better custom-made frames fit together well and present a neat, sophisticated appearance.

Small table frames
A wide assortment of table frames is available for displaying small prints. These frames are usually constructed of wood, metal, or ceramic, and they are sometimes covered with leather, caning, or fabric. (See the photograph that opens this chapter.)

You can present your photographs in small table frames either alone or organized into an attractive arrangement of individually framed photographs. By periodically changing some or all of the photographs in the arrangement you can present visitors with a rotating exhibition of your work.

Traditionally, table frames have been used for displaying family portraits, but there is no reason why table frames cannot be used to display any photograph you would like others to appreciate.

CLIP FRAMES
By virtue of their simplicity, clip frames allow a viewer's attention to focus on the print rather than on its mounting.

MOUNTING TECHNIQUES

If you expect to dry mount only occasionally, or if you want to avoid the purchase of an expensive dry-mounting press, you can mount your prints using an ordinary electric iron. Hot water will damage your print, so be sure to use the iron on its "dry" rather than "steam" setting. Better yet, empty all water from the iron before turning it on.

Start by preheating your iron to a moderate, dry temperature and trimming the mounting tissue to the size of the print, then follow the procedures described at right.

MOUNTING PRINTS

The mounting technique you use with a particular print is a matter of personal preference as long as the adhesive involved is appropriate for the materials being joined. However, you should always bear in mind that you may need to strike a balance between the ease of a particular technique and the degree of permanence you are seeking. Many papers, adhesives, and even frames contain acids which will cause the image on a print or the paper itself to deteriorate over the years. If you want to preserve a print for decades – or centuries – you must sacrifice the convenience of some of the easier techniques for the permanence provided by acid-free mounting materials and methods.

Dry mounting

Dry mounting is permanent, clean in that it provides a smooth mount, and time tested. In dry mounting you place a special tissue between the print and the mounting board, then apply heat to form the bond.

Resin-coated (RC) and Cibachrome papers can be dry mounted, but you must monitor the temperature carefully to prevent the edges from curling or the print from being completely destroyed. The ideal heat source is a special dry-mounting press, but you can also use a household iron, if necessary. If you use a laundry iron, however, you must learn the best temperature by trial and error, and until you do, in all likelihood scorched prints will be an occasional occurrence. Even with a mounting press, temperature control is difficult. Ademco make a special low temperature tissue for Resin-Coated (RC) papers.

Wet mounting

Wet mounting, a permanent and time-tested, if somewhat messy, process, entails the use of wet glue as the bonding agent between print and mounting board. Wet mounting is the only mounting method practical for use with murals. If executed with care, wet mounting will provide you with a smoothly mounted print and a very permanent bond. For fibre-base paper mounted on porous surfaces such as wood, Masonite, or cardboard, use white glue diluted with water to make it smooth and thin enough to apply with a brush. For RC paper, or if the print is to be mounted on a nonporous

Small, acid-free tapes are used as hinges to mount a print. Available in most art supply stores, these hinges are easy to remove and make changing a mount a simple task.

surface such as metal or plastic, use a contact cement (but beware of fumes).

To make a wet mount:
1. *Prepare mounting board* slightly smaller than the size of the print.
2. *Apply thin, smooth layer of diluted white glue or undiluted contact cement* (as appropriate) with a paintbrush to both the back of the print and the mount surface.
3. *Wait* for the two surfaces to become sticky.
4. *Position print* very carefully above, but not touching the mounting surface.
5. *Lower print* very carefully onto the mounting surface (no repositioning is possible once the surfaces touch).
6. *Smooth out any bubbles* using a roller (available from art supply stores), working from the middle of the print toward the outside edges.
7. *Trim print flush* with the edge of the mounting board, or neatly glue and wrap the edge of the print around the edge of the board.

Spray adhesive

Spray adhesives are very fast to use but do not produce a permanent bond. Also, the chemicals in the spray can react with the print and damage it as time passes. Use spray adhesives when constructing a temporary exhibit, when producing "paste-ups" to be submitted to a printer, or when you know you will need to reposition the prints later. If you want the prints to be easy to remove, allow the adhesive to dry for a while before you mount them. (Solvents are available to facilitate print removal.)

To use a spray adhesive:
1. *Trim print* to size.
2. *Lay print face down on sheet of newspaper.*
3. *Spray back of print* with adhesive.
4. *Lay print in position* on the mounting surface.
5. *Smooth print* with a roller.

Cold mounting

Two different types of cold mount are available: one that sandwiches an adhesive-coated sheet between the print and the mount (e.g. Seal and 3M's), and another that involves transferring a layer of adhesive from a sheet of special paper onto the back of the print. This has the advantage of not adding to the thickness of the mount and of avoiding any acidity an intermediate sheet might contain; in both methods, however, there may be acids present in the adhesive itself.

To make the type of cold mount that does not leave an intermediate sheet between the print and the mount, see p. 151.

Some dry-mounting tissues work by inserting a sheet of paper, coated on both sides with adhesive, between the print and the surface of the mounting material. Peeling away the tissue's protective papers exposes the adhesive.

Hinge mounts consist of small strips of acid-free paper or cloth folded in half and attached to both the back of a print and the surface on which the print is to be mounted. Because hinge mounts are so small, they minimize the amount of adhesive on the print and therefore decrease the likelihood of the print's being damaged by chemicals in the adhesive. Hinge mounts have the added virtue of allowing easy removal of the prints, should that later become necessary.

1. **Dry-mounting tissue**
2. **Wet-mounting adhesives**
3. **Cold-mounting adhesive sheets**
4. **Spray-mounting adhesive**
5. **Acid-free tape**

To make a cold mount "sandwich" using an intermediate adhesive sheet:
1. *Position print* on top of the adhesive carrier sheet.
2. *Peel protective paper* carefully away from one side of the adhesive sheet so that the adhesive comes in contact with the print.
3. *Smooth adhesive sheet* with a roller.
4. *Trim adhesive paper* down to the size of the print
5. *Peel away protective paper* from the other side of the adhesive sheet.
6. *Affix print* to the mounting board.
7. *Smooth print* with a roller.

Hinge mounting

Small, acid-free tapes (available from art supply stores) that are cut into small strips, folded in half, and used as hinges constitute the safest mounting method of all with respect to print preservation. Hinges are easy to remove, and they make changing a mount a simple task. Aside from being free from acid, they have the additional advantage of bringing the smallest area of mounting surface in contact with the print, compared to other mounting methods.

To make a hinge mount:
1. *Cut mat* with an opening small enough to cover the edges of the print.
2. *Cut at least two 2″ or 3″ (5 or 8 cm) lengths of acid-free tape.*
3. *Fold tapes* in half, widthwise.
4. *Affix one flap of each "hinge"* onto the back of the print.
5. *Position print* over the mounting board.
6. *Press print* into place on the board.
7. *Secure print* by covering it with the mat prepared in step 1.
8. *Frame* (optional).

DRY MOUNTING WITH AN IRON

1. *Gather materials.* **You will need an iron, a ruler (a centre-finding ruler is best), a cutting blade, a pencil, a print to be mounted, dry-mounting tissue cut to the size of the print, and a mounting board cut to whatever size you want.**

2. *Position print on mounting board.* **Use your eye to locate the print where you want it, then position the print precisely by measuring with the ruler to achieve even borders. Mark the locations of the top edge and one side edge of the print on the mounting board with a light pencil line.**

3. *"Tack" mounting tissue to print.* **Turn the print face down and place the mounting tissue on top of the print. "Tack" the mounting tissue to the back of the print by tracing an "X" pattern between the corners with the tip of a dry iron set to a medium temperature.**

4. *Mount print.* **Position the print face up on the mounting board, using the pencil lines as guides. Cover the print with a piece of clean paper, then run the iron across the entire surface of the print. Work from the centre outward to prevent scorching.**

COLD MOUNTING

The type of cold mount in which a sheet of paper with adhesive on both sides is inserted between a print and its mounting board is described on p. 149. A different type of cold mount that does not add such a sheet between the print and its mount is illustrated at right. Which of the products you use is primarily a matter of personal preference, although the type shown here has the advantage of allowing position adjustments any time before the final burnishing step.

1. *Position print on mounting board.* Referring to the right-hand photograph at the top of the previous page, mark the locations of the top edge and one side edge of your print on the mounting board.
2. *Transfer adhesive to print.* Cut the adhesive carrier sheet from a mounting kit such as the one shown above to the same size as your print. Peel away the protective paper from the adhesive carrier sheet, then position the sheet against the back of the print as shown. Next, firmly burnish the entire back surface of the carrier paper.

4. *Mount print.* Position the print face up on the mounting board, using the pencil lines as guides. Cover the print with the protective paper you removed earlier, and firmly burnish the print onto the mounting board.

3. *Expose adhesive.* Remove the adhesive carrier sheet carefully, leaving behind a layer of adhesive on the back of the print.

HOW TO CUT A MOUNT

One popular mounting technique involves surrounding a print with an attractive border. You produce the border by carefully cutting a window in a special cardboard (available from art supply stores); you then position the cardboard frame so that it surrounds the print and holds it flat. You can either insert the print-mat combination in a frame or mount it on an uncut board using an appropriate technique.

Standard Mounts

To determine the dimensions of the borders on your mount you must make an aesthetic decision that will vary from print to print. However, you should pay close attention to the relative widths of the borders if you want your photographs to look their best.

In a standard, traditional mount, the two side borders and top border are all equal in width, while the bottom border is approximately one-third wider. However, do not feel forced to use the standard proportions exclusively. Other types of border dimensions you might consider are illustrated on p. 157.

Equipment

Window mounts look best if the window through which the print is viewed has been cut with an edge bevelled at an angle. Art supply stores sell various cutting devices, some of which are quite elaborate and expensive. Fortunately, one of the simplest and least expensive, is perfectly adequate. To use the cutter most effectively, you will also need a T-square ruler (preferably metal), a C-clamp, a push-pin, a large sheet of scrap cardboard to place under the mat while you cut, and a firm surface on which to work. Useful, but not absolutely necessary, is a "centre-finding" ruler.

PREPARATIONS
1. *Gather materials.*
   Metal T-Square ruler
   Centre-finding ruler
   Cutter
   Push-pin
   Mounting board
   Backing cardboard
   Print to be mounted
2. *Determine actual dimensions of window* you will be cutting. (Be certain that the mount will overlap the photograph by at least $\frac{1}{8}''$ (3 mm) on all sides).
3. *Adjust blade on cutter.* Follow the manufacturer's instructions. Set the blade to the angle you want and to the correct depth for the thickness of the board you are using.

MARKING THE WINDOW OUTLINE
4. *Centre centre-finding ruling horizontally* on the face of the mount.
5. *Centre print horizontally* underneath the ruler.
6. *Measure distance from left edge of image area to left edge of mount.* (Be sure your measurement includes the amount the mount will overlap the print. Do not make the measurement from the very edge of the printing paper.)
7. *Adjust position of both rulers* as shown above so that they intersect where the measurement on each equals the distance you determined in the previous step.
8. *Mark Intersection* with the push-pin.
9. *Repeat steps 6 and 7* on the other side of the mount.
10. *Measure straight down* (using the T-square ruler) from both pinholes a distance equal to the vertical dimension of the window, and mark with additional pinholes.

CUTTING THE MOUNT

The first step in cutting a mount is to determine the border proportions you want. Lay the photograph to be framed on top of the cardboard, and shift the photograph around until you locate the position you like best. The instructions at right are written for a mount with the top and side borders all equal in width, but you may decide that for a particular photograph you prefer the widths of the top and bottom borders to be different from the width of the side borders.

The photographs here illustrate how to measure and cut a window *using a centre-finding ruler.* If you do not have a centre-finding ruler, you will have to determine where the corners of the window in the mount will be. Proceed as follows:

1. *Decide on exact dimensions* of the window in the mount, keeping in mind that the mount should overlap the print by at least $\frac{1}{8}''$ (.3 cm) on each side.
2. *Turn the mount face down.*
3. *Locate mount's centre* by drawing diagonal lines between the opposite corners.
4. *Locate and mark right and left edges of window with lines,* making certain that both borders are equal in width.
5. *Locate and mark upper edge of window* with a line. Usually you will want to make the upper border equal in width to the side borders.
6. *Locate and mark lower edge of window with line.* Usually, you will want the lower border to be about one-third wider than the other borders.
7. *Push pin through mount at each of four corners of window* in order to transfer the location of the corners to the front of the mount.
8. *Continue with procedures outlined at right,* commencing with step 11.

CUTTING THE MOUNT

11. *Double-check angle and depth of cutter blade.*
12. *Push cutter blade firmly into either of two pinholes* nearest to you.
13. *Position T-square against side of cutter and along line of cut.* **Make certain that along the line of cut the distance from both pinholes to the T-square is equal.**
14. *Clamp T-square in place.* **(If you try to hand-hold the T-square, its position will shift during the cut.)**
15. *Position hands as shown above.*
16. *Push cutter firmly along,* **from the near hole to the far hole.**
17. *Repeat steps 13 through 17* **on the remaining sides of the mount.**

MOUNTING AND FRAMING

18. *Position print* on the mounting board.
19. *Lay frame over print.* **Make certain that the borders overlap the print on all sides.**
20. *Remove frame* **without disturbing the position of the print.**
21. *Mark edges of print* on the mounting board with a pencil.
22. *Mount print* on the mounting board. Use whichever of the mounting techniques mentioned earlier in this chapter is appropriate for your materials, the way you want your print to look, and the degree of permanence you want.

FRAMING THE PRINT

CUSTOM FRAMING

Any time you need a frame of other than standard dimensions, you will have to make your own (or have one made to order, an expensive alternative). Customising a frame is a relatively easy task, however, if you use the strip frame kits pictured at right.

You will need to buy two separate kits to make one frame, since frame edges are sold two to a package. In deciding what lengths to buy, you must establish the approximate dimensions you want the frame to be, then select packages containing edge strips cut as nearly as possible to those lengths. The hardware for connecting the frame edges is included in the packages, but you will need to purchase a sheet of glass or Plexiglas of the proper dimensions. Glass does not scratch as easily as plastic, but it is more difficult to cut, breaks more easily, and is heavier. The choice of which to use is a matter of personal preference.

Usually, you will not need a custom frame unless you have mounted your print in a manner such that it requires a frame of non-standard dimensions, as when you cover a print with a mount. Even with a mount, you will probably need to back your print with a piece of cardboard to add rigidity and to make sure the print fits snugly in the frame.

CUSTOM FRAMING

Gather materials.
Four frame edges plus hardware.
A sheet of glass or acrylic plastic (Plexiglas).
Picture-hanging wire with mounting clips.
The print, mounted on a mount.
Backing board.
Screwdriver.

2. *Connect three sides via two corners.* **Slide the L-shaped connectors into the slots in the edge sections, as shown, and tighten the screws.**

3. *Slip glass, matted print and backing board into frame.* **Make certain the combination fits snugly in the frame.**

4. *Attach wire mounting clips. Attach fourth edge.* **Slide the wire mounting clips into place and secure. Attach the remaining corner hardware to the fourth edge before mounting it. Be sure the wire is securely attached.**

Clips such as these hold together a "sandwich" made of glass or Plexiglas, a matted print, and a stiff backing board which adds rigidity and enables the lip to grip the sandwich firmly. To assemble such a frame, you construct the sandwich and then press the clips onto the top and bottom edges as shown. Once you apply tension to the string that links the clips, the assembly will be ready for hanging by means of the slot in the upper clip.

A similar type of frame uses four corner clips instead of two edge clips. Both edge clips and corner clips are available clear or coloured, in plastic or metal.

WOOD STRIP BACKINGS

Flush- and wrap-mounted prints often look best if they are hung to stand approximately 1″ (2.5 cm) out from the wall. Two wood strips attached to the back of the mounting board in the manner shown above serve both to create a space between the wall and board and to re-inforce the rigidity of the board.

Attach the wood strips parallel to the top and bottom edges of the backing board with glue, but far enough from the edges for the viewer not to be able to see the strips when the print is hung. Centre the strips left to right so their weight will be evenly distributed. To mount the assembly on the wall, simply hook the uppermost wood strip over a nail.

MOUNTING VARIATIONS

You can create an unusual and often pleasing effect by making multiple prints of a subject, then mounting them together. In the photograph above, the twelve images are mounted side by side on a sheet of high-quality art paper using a spray adhesive, and the whole assembly is matted together. This technique provides an interesting method for making a small print into a large display.

As suggested earlier, mounts need not always be cut using traditional measurements and border proportions. For example, sometimes a vertical print will look best on a horizontal board. Or, you may find that the impact of a particularly small print is enhanced by surrounding it with a very large mount. And nowhere is it decreed that the print must always be centered left to right. Use your imagination, but always keep in mind that a non-standard mount enhances a photograph only if it is serving a specific, aesthetic function that provides a reason for deviating from the traditional norms.

One caution about mount variations: if you are planning to display a *collection* of prints, they should all be given the same treatment – especially if you are planning to present them as part of a formal exhibition.

Some photographs are better left unmounted. The photograph at left is mounted so that it "bleeds" all the way to the edge of the frame for added impact.

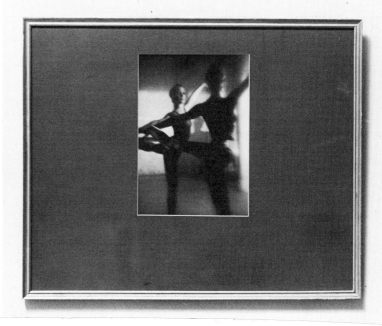

Unusually wide borders can be effective if you want to direct attention to a small print.

The shape of the mount need not necessarily echo the shape of the print it surrounds. Here a vertical print is mounted and framed in a horizontal format.

SOME MOUNTING FORMATS

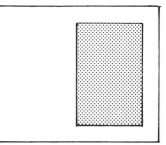

STORING YOUR TRANSPARENCIES AND NEGATIVES

Authorities disagree over how long a photographic image will last. Some maintain that a transparency will begin to deteriorate after being exposed for as little as 60 seconds under a 250-watt projector bulb. Others maintain that a carefully processed and stored black and white negative will last for 3,000 years. Both contentions may be correct considering that they deal with extreme conditions, but the most common estimates of the ability of an image to survive range from 50 to 100 years. Since some of the earliest photographs taken are still in existence and are therefore about 150 years old, it seems safe to conclude that properly kept black and white photographic materials have the potential at least to outlive their creators and survive for the enjoyment of other generations. Colour films have not been in existence long enough to arrive at firm conclusions.

In theory, photographs prepared using the newer materials and processes should survive as well as their predecessors. In fact, no one yet knows for certain whether they will.

What *is* known are the factors that contribute to image deterioration. Paper, cardboard, glue, and unsealed wood all give off fumes that react with and tarnish the silver granules on film and paper. Enviromental pollutants, especially sulphur compounds, cause images to deteriorate. High temperature, high humidity, and constant exposure to light can encourage mould to grow or an image to fade. Physical abuse can also play a part; pressure on the face of a transparency caused by being under a large stack of other transparencies; oil from fingerprints; and dust or grit all can take a toll.

Glassine and paper envelopes
For years, glassine envelopes were the preferred method for storing negatives. More recently, it has been discovered that the glue on the envelopes is harmful. However, acid-free paper envelopes are available and safe.

Plastic slide trays and cubes
Slides that you want to be able to view easily and often can be safely stored in plastic slide trays and cubes, ready for projection. Remember, however, that repeated or prolonged exposure to the intense light of a projector bulb will cause the image on the transparency to fade.

Conditions. Because prints may contain residual processing chemicals within the paper, or acids may be present in mounting materials, prints are more likely to deteriorate over the years than are transparencies and negatives. There-

fore, fundamental to the preservation of prints are the archival processing methods described in Chapter Four. Beyond that, any storage system you choose for all materials – negatives, slides, and prints – must strike a balance between how much protection you want your photographic materials to enjoy and how accessible you need them to be.

Temperature. For maximum protection, store your negatives at a temperature as close to 21°C (70°F) as you can maintain.

Humidity. Relative humidity should remain in the 15%-40% range.

Light. When not being displayed, protect all materials from light, especially sunlight.

Fumes. All materials should be protected from contact with corrosive fumes to the greatest extent practical.

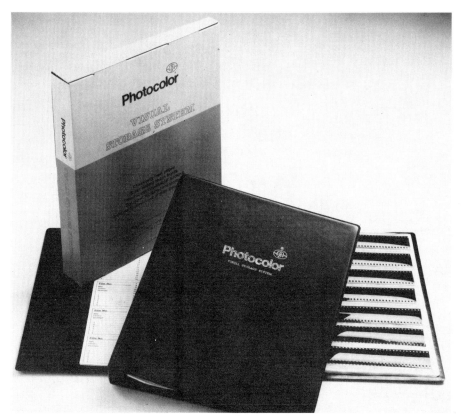

An easy way to store negatives and transparencies is to insert them in plastic sheets and organize the sheets in loose-leaf folders.

If you make a contact print of each sheet of stored negatives, you can include the print so that it lies facing the negatives from which it was prepared.

STORAGE CONTAINERS

Plastic sheets

The plastic sheets in which negatives are stored consist of slots which hold the strips of film. Usually, you can store an entire 36-exposure roll on one sheet. These sheets allow you both to view the negatives and to make a contact print without having to remove the film from the sheet.

The plastic sheets in which transparencies are stored comes in two varieties. The sheets made of polyethylene or cellulose acetate act as frames for each individual transparency, with slots for twenty transparencies on each sheet. The drawback of these sheets is that they leave the surfaces of the transparencies unprotected from dust, grit, and fingerprints. If you use overlay sheets for protection, it becomes difficult to retrieve individual transparencies.

Another type of sheet consists of individual envelopes for each transparency which completely enclose the transparencies, but since these sheets are not made of inert plastic, over the years some harm may come to the transparencies they hold. Moreover, if the film itself comes into contact with the plastic for a long period of time, the image may be ruined. Therefore, this type of sheet is best used only for glass slides you will be removing regularly.

Be careful not to store plastic sheets one on top of another in large stacks, or else the negatives or transparencies on the bottom may be damaged. A better method is to store the sheets vertically in hanging files or loose-leaf notebooks.

Boxes

Negatives, transparencies, and prints should only be stored in boxes that do not radiate harmful fumes. Only boxes made of specially prepared acid-free cardboard, or wood that has been covered by a layer of thoroughly dried paint, are safe to use. Metal boxes and filing cabinets are usually safe.

Proper storage of transparencies is important for their preservation. Slide trays, metal storage boxes, and acetate sleeves all meet different organizational and viewing needs, but each is effective in its own way.

The carousel slide carriage shown in this modern audio-visual apparatus can be used to store slides safely, but it can be very expensive when a large collection is involved.

APPENDIX

Liquid and Capacity Measurement

Gallons	Quarts	Pints	Fluid Ounces	Fluid Drams	Ml	Centilitres	Litres
1	4	8	160	1024	4546	454.6	4.546
.25	1	2	40	256	1173	117.3	1.173
.125	.5	1	20	128	568.25	56.8	.568
.0078	.03125	.0625	1	8	28.41	2.841	.02841
.000976	.0039	.0078	.125	1	3.551	.3551	.003697

Length

Yards	Feet	Inches	Millimetres	Centimetres	Metres
.0011	.0033	.039	1	.1	.001
.011	.033	.394	10	1	.01
.028	.083	1	25.4	2.54	.025
.333	1	12	305	30.5	.305
1	3	36	914	91.4	.914
1.09	3.28	39.4	1000	100	1

Avoirdupois to Metric

Pounds	Ounces	Grains	Grams	Kilograms
1	16	7000	453.60	.45
.0625	1	437.50	28.35	.02835
—	—	1	.06	—
—	.035	15.43	1	.001
2.205	35.27	15432	1000	1

Temperature Conversion
$$°C = (°F - 32) \times 5/9$$
$$°F = (°C \times 9/5) + 32$$

Dry Capacity Measurement
1 pint = 33.60 cubic inches = 550 millilitres = 0.550 litres

Liquid Measure
1 quart = 32 ounces = 946.4 millilitres = .9464 litre
1 ounce = 29.60 millilitres = .0296 litre
1 litre = 1000 millilitres = 33.81 ounces = 1.057 quarts

Surface Areas
80 square inches = surface of one 36-exposure
35mm roll, one 120 roll film approx.
or one 8″ x 10″ (20 x 25 cm) sheet

The life and strength of mixed chemicals can be affected by the way they are mixed and replenished and by the temperature at which they are stored. If you notice that your negatives are not showing the density and contrast you expect, depleted chemicals could be the problem. Develop good mixing technique from the start, and you will save yourself aggravation in the future. Maintain accurate records of when chemicals were mixed, how many rolls they have been employed to process, and how many times the chemicals have been replenished. With such records you can more easily identify the source of a problem when it occurs. If you follow the procedures outlined below, you will not only extend the life of your chemicals, but you will also develop a skill that is the hallmark of the darkroom expert: the ability to produce predictable results, consistently.

AGITATION

The primary agent in chemical deterioriation is oxidation, that is, the action of oxygen on chemicals, especially on developers. The way you mix chemicals can affect the amount of oxygen introduced into a solution. The mixing tools sold in camera stores are specifically designed to prevent excess agitation from occurring at the top of a liquid, where the chemical meets the air. By vigorously agitating the solution only at the bottom, you are mixing the chemicals in a region where no air is present. Your goal is to mix the chemicals sufficiently to dissolve all of the powder into the liquid but without so disturbing the surface that air is introduced.

MIXING TEMPERATURES

When mixing chemicals, be careful to maintain the chemical temperature within the range recommended by the manufacturer. If you mix at too low a temperature, the chemical may not fully dissolve; if you mix at too high a temperature, the chemical may decompose.

Before using a chemical for processing, check to be certain that the temperature has fallen to the proper range.

WATER

Ordinary tap water is suitable for mixing chemicals unless the water has an excessively high sulphur content. Too much sulphur causes fogged negatives. If you suspect sulphur contamination (a rare occurrence), you can test for it by mixing a batch of chemicals with distilled or spring water to see if this eliminates the problem. If not, the culprit may be chemical exhaustion or some other contamination.

STORAGE TEMPERATURE

Maintain storage temperatures between 10°C (50°F) and 32°C (90°F) because the shelf life of mixed chemicals can be altered by excessively high or low storage tempera-

tures. Below 10°C (50°F), dissolved chemicals may start to crystallize. Above 32°C (90°F), the rate of oxidation increases substantially, and the life of the chemical may decrease from months or weeks to only days.

REPLENISHING

Some chemicals are used once, usually in diluted form, then discarded. This procedure ensures fresh chemistry and consistent results each time you process, but diluted chemicals do not work as fast as concentrated chemicals, which are more convenient to use. Moreover, you can use full-strength chemistry over and over again by replenishing the depleted chemical after each use. If a chemical (often a developer) can be replenished, its manufacturer will usually provide replenishment instructions. In some cases, however, a special replenisher is made by a different manufacturer. If you do not have either replenishment instructions or a special replenisher, then follow the procedure below for chemicals designed to be used in concentrated form.

Add to the used chemical 1 oz (28.4 ml) of fresh stock solution for each 80 square inches (2 m²) of film processed (80 square inches = one 36-exposure roll of 35mm film). If 1 oz does not bring the solution back to its original volume, then add additional fresh stock solution. Do not continue replenishing indefinitely, however, since a chemical builds more and more residual silver and sludge each time it is replenished.

Should you notice that film being processed in replenished chemicals is showing reduced density, add more stock solution to the used solution, even if you have to discard some of the used solution to maintain the correct volume. If your negatives start to show increased density, then use less replenisher. If using less replenisher results in an insufficient volume of liquid, dilute the replenisher 1:1 with water. Keep in mind, however, that weak negatives may signal an exhausted solution. When in doubt, replace the chemistry.

TONING

Print *toning* can serve both to alter the colour of an image and, by replacing some of the silver in the image with a more chemically inert substance, to help preserve the image. Sepia, brown, blue, red, and other toner shades are primarily intended for altering the colour of an image, with protection being a secondary consideration. Selenium and gold toners, on the other hand, are excellent for improving print longevity but have little or no effect on colour.

Sepia toner. This toner produces a warm, brownish tone on black paper. It comes in two solutions: bleach and redeveloper.

Kodak brown toner. This produces a browner tone than sepia toner on black and white paper. It comes in one solution.

Gold protective toner. Use this toner for the greatest archival preservation of a photographic image. It has little or no effect on image colour.

Selenium toner. This is a less expensive and more commonly used substitute for gold toner in archival printing. It produces a reddish brown colour when used on some papers and no noticeable colour change on others.

SPOTTING PRINTS

No matter how carefully you clean your negatives, some dust spots will inevitably appear on your prints. To cover the spots you will need to have on hand a variety of high-quality, fine-point artist's brushes, ranging in size from 000 to 1. Also, you should purchase Photocolor Photographic Dye print retouching colours.

To spot a print, mix the colours according to the general instructions provided by the colours' manufacturer for the type of paper you are using. You will have to experiment to obtain the best mixture of retouching colours to match the tones surrounding the spot you want to retouch.

Apply the colours with a semi-dry brush in very thin layers rather than in a single, thick layer. To avoid accidentally ending up with a spot that is too dark, mix your first layers a little lighter in tone than you think is correct and keep darkening the tone in subsequent layers until the match is perfect. In the best spotting jobs, the colour has been applied as little dots that approximate the grain shown by the image.

If you make a mistake and are using RC paper, you can sometimes wash the entire print in water and start over.

TEST FOR FIXER EXHAUSTION

Periodically you should check to see if your fixer has remained at full working strength. To test a hypo-type fixer, add 2 drops of hypo test liquid. If the drops turn white, the fixer should be discarded. If they remain clear, the fixer is still usable. To test a high-speed fixer, take out 1-2 oz (28-56 ml) of the fixer to be tested, add 1 or 2 drops of the tester and shake the mixture. If the solution turns milky white, the fixer is exhausted and should be discarded. If the solution clears, the fixer is still usable.

TEST FOR HYPO

Because the presence of residual hypo in a finished print can ultimately lead to its deterioration, you may want to test your prints during the wash period to see if all hypo has been eliminated. The procedure is to apply 1 drop of Kodak hypo test solution HT-2 to a test print that has been wiped free of water. By comparing the colour produced on the print to the sample colours on the Kodak Hypo Estimator, you can determine the amount of residual hypo present on the print.

CLEANING

The stains from the developer which form in the bottom of processing trays can easily be removed by using Paterson

Tank, Dish and Rack Cleaner. You dilute the concentrated solution with three parts water, swirl the mixture around in the soiled dish, and then discard the solution. You can repeat the process if necessary to remove stubborn stains. Afterwards, wash the cleaned surface with water. The solution works well on metal, rubber, polyethylene, polystyrene, and porcelain dishes, but be careful to rinse porcelain dishes promptly to prevent the surface from being etched by the cleaner.

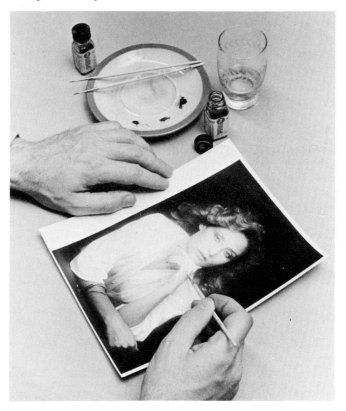

SPOTTING PRINTS

GLOSSARY

Acetic acid – A chemical used to stop the activity of a developer quickly and completely. (See Stop bath.)

Agitation – The process of inducing movement in liquid chemicals for the purpose of insuring that chemical reactions occur at a uniform rate.

Aperture – The adjustable opening in a lens diaphragm through which light passes. (See also Stop.)

Archival printing – Special procedures designed to forestall print deterioration by removing all harmful residual chemicals from a print.

ASA – A number rating applied to a film to characterize the film's sensitivity to light (See ISO.)

Bleach – A chemical used in processing to remove silver granules.

Burning-in – A technique used in printing whereby a portion of the light being projected onto the printing paper is allowed to strike the paper for a longer time than the rest of the light. In prints made from negatives (black and white or colour), the burnt-in area is darkened. In prints made from transparencies, the burnt-in area is lightened.

Cassette – The metal or plastic cylinder in which 35mm film is sold and stored, and from which the film must be removed before processing.

Changing bag – A light-tight cloth bag within which light-sensitive materials (unprocessed film or printing paper) can be handled while room lights are on or sunlight is present.

Clearing agent – A chemical that reduces washing time by rapidly removing fixer from film or prints.

Cold-light enlarger – An enlarger in which the light source is made of gas-filled tubes that produce far less heat than tungsten bulbs or fluorescent lamps.

Cold mounting – A method that does not require the application of heat to affix a print to a mount surface. The adhesive is usually layered onto a sheet of paper and either sandwiched, along with the paper, between the print and the mount or transferred from the paper onto the print itself.

Colour analyser – An electronic device that measures the constituent colours in a projected image and indicates the filtration adjustments required to produce correct colour balance in a print made from the image.

Colour balance – The relationship between colours in a print. When colour balance is correct, the colours in a print closely or exactly reproduce the colours in the original scene. Colour balance is unaffected by the colours contained in the light source used to produce or view an image, by the inherent characteristics of the film, and by the characteristics of the particular emulsion batch on which the image is photographically reproduced.

Colour calculator – A device containing many combinations of filters and filter densities, through which a colour image is projected to make a test print. By studying the test print, it is possible to determine the filter combination that will produce an image with correct colour balance. (See Colour balance.)

Colour developer – A chemical used in colour-reversal processing that attaches coloured dyes to developing images.

Colour mask – A tint or a tinted layer on film that serves to reduce contrast in prints made from the film. The colour mask gives colour negatives their orangish cast.

Colour reversal – The process whereby the negative image initially formed on the film is changed to a positive image so that the transparency can be viewed directly. Colour reversal also takes place on colour printing paper when a positive print is made from a transparency.

Colour-reversal film – Film on the surface of which colour is changed so that a positive colour image is formed. (Colour-reversal film is commonly referred to as transparency or slide film.)

Colour temperature – A way of describing the colour produced by a light source. Each type of colour film responds most accurately to light of a particular colour temperature.

Compensating developer – A developer used for processing film exposed to high-contrast subjects. The developer decreases the overall contrast in the negatives but does not significantly affect the separation of tones in highlight and shadow areas.

Complementary colours – The colours resulting from the mixture of equal amounts of any two of the primary colours. Red mixed with green produces yellow; red mixed with blue produces magenta; green mixed with blue produces cyan. These are also called *Secondary colours*. (See Primary colours.)

Contact print – A print made by laying film directly on top of a sheet of printing paper, then projecting white light through the film to produce an image on the paper. Most often, contact prints are made of an entire negative film at once, to facilitate evaluation of the individual frames on the roll.

Contact printer – A device designed to hold film flat against a sheet of printing paper so that a good contact print can be made.

Condenser enlarger – An enlarger characterized by the inclusion of lenses designed to produce sharp images with high contrast. Condenser enlargers are usually best suited to black and white printing, but they can be adapted to colour use.

Contrast – The range of light intensities contained in a scene or a photographic image. Scenes or images showing a narrow range of light intensities are said to be *low contrast*. Scenes or images showing a wide range of light intensities are said to be *high contrast* or *contrasty*.

Contrast grade – A designation of the range of light intensities a particular sheet of printing paper will produce. The grades run from 0 (low contrast) to 5 (high contrast). The No. 2 paper is considered "normal" and will reproduce more or less exactly the range of light intensities in a negative of average (not extreme) contrast.

Contrasty – See Contrast.

Copy negative – A negative produced by either photographing a print or duplicating another negative.

Cropping – Adjusting the borders of a print to exclude unwanted elements from it. Also referred to as 'Trimming'.

Cyan – One of the complementary colours that form the foundation to the subtractive method of colour production. Cyan filters block red light but allow green light and blue light to pass.

Depth of field – The range of distances in front of a lens that will be rendered in sharp focus by the lens. The depth of field of a lens increases as the size of the aperture to which the lens is set decreases. (See Aperture.)

Developer – Chemicals that convert silver halide crystals that have been exposed to light into metallic silver, thereby converting a latent photographic image into a developed image. (See Latent image.)

Density – An indication of the relative thickness of a developed image on a frame of film. "Dense" negatives appear dark to the eye and require relatively long exposures to form an image on paper. "Thin" negatives appear light to the eye and require relatively short exposures to form an image on paper. An "optimally dense" negative requires moderate exposures and shows better shadow and highlight detail than dense or thin negatives.

Diaphragm – A mechanical device built into photographic lenses which permits the size of the lens aperture to be adjusted. Rotating a ring on the outside of the lens causes the diaphragm to change

to a different aperture or stop. (See Aperture.)

Dichroic enlarger – An enlarger characterized by the presence of dichroic filters in the enlarger head. Dichroic enlargers are usually best-suited for colour printing or for black and white applications where an image is desired that is somewhat less distinct than that produced by a condenser enlarger. (See dichroic filters.)

Dichroic filters – Subtractive sharp cut colour filters which "interfere" with the light coming from an enlarger lamp. The further a particular filter extends into the light path, the greater the intensity of that colour in the light emerging from the enlarger head.

Dodging – A technique whereby light from the enlarger is partially blocked during part of the exposure time of a print. In prints made from negatives (black and white or colour) the dodged area is lightened. In prints made from transparencies, the dodged area is darkened.

Double exposure – A technique whereby two separate images are exposed on a single sheet of printing paper.

Drum processor – A plastic tube in which prints can be processed. Special end caps permit processing chemicals to be introduced and removed without light being admitted.

Dry-mounting press – A device that uses heat and pressure to affix a print to a mounting surface.

Dry-mounting tissue – Tissue that is placed between a print and the surface on which it is to be mounted. Heat applied to the print causes an adhesive bond to form.

Dry side – The portions of a darkroom devoted to exposing, but not processing, prints.

Dye couplers – Chemicals contained within the emulsion layers of colour films and papers which, in conjunction with colour developers, result in the production of colour images. (See Colour developer.)

Emulsion – The layer or layers on film or printing paper that contain light-sensitive chemicals. After processing, the emulsion layer (or layers, in the case of colour materials) contains the developed image.

Emulsion number – A number, applied by the manufacturer of a roll of film or a box

of printing paper, that identifies the emulsion batch from which the film or paper was made. The emulsion number is especially important in colour processing because each emulsion batch responds somewhat differently to colours.

Enlargement – A print that is larger than the negative or slide from which it was made.

Enlarger – A device having a light source and lens to project the image from a negative or transparency onto a sheet of printing paper.

Enlarger head – The portion of an enlarger that contains its light source and to which its lens is attached. (See Enlarger lens.)

Enlarger lens – A lens designed to project a distortion-free, flat image onto a sheet of printing paper. In 35mm photography, the enlarger lens should have a focal length of approximately 50mm.

Enlarger timer – A timer into which an enlarger can be plugged and which automatically turns off the enlarger after a set interval of time.

Exposure – The particular combinations of lens aperture (*f*/stop) and exposure time that will allow the proper amount of light to strike film or printing paper to record the best possible image. (See Aperture; *f*-stop.)

Exposure latitude – The range of exposures, including over-exposures and under-exposures, that produce at least some detail in the highlights and shadow areas of an image. The exposure latitude of black and white film is approximately seven stops; of colour film, approximately five stops.

Exposure meter – A device that measures the intensity of light and indicates the combinations of lens aperture and exposure time that will result in a correct exposure of a light-sensitive material (film or paper). Camera meters cannot be used for determining darkroom exposures without the addition of special accessories.

Ferrotyping – A process whereby glossy prints are dried on a sheet of heated chrome-plated steel to increase the amount of gloss shown by the print.

Fibre-base paper – Printing paper that has not been coated by a resin to retard its absorption of moisture.

Film speed – A measurement of a film's sensitivity to light, usually designated by an ASA rating or an ISO rating. The higher the number, the faster (or the more sensitive to light) the film.

Filter – A clear or translucent piece of glass, gelatin, or acetate which is placed between a source of light and a piece of light-sensitive material to alter the light in a predetermined fashion. Some filters affect colour, others absorb unwanted radiation, and still others modify the way an image appears.

Filter, colour-compensating (CC) – High-quality but fragile gelatin filters that add controlled amounts of colour to light. Because of their high optical purity, CC filters can be placed below the lens of an enlarger without significantly distorting the quality of the image the enlarger projects. (See Filter density.)

Filter, colour-printing (CP) – Acetate filters that add controlled amounts of colour to light. Because CP filters contain optical impurities, they must be placed *above* the negative or slide in an enlarger or else the image projected by the enlarger will be distorted. (See Filter density.)

Filter density – A measurement of the intensity of the colour present in a colour filter. Colour-compensating and colour printing filters are sold in multiples of five density units.

Filter drawer – A compartment of a condenser enlarger designed to accommodate filters. Filter drawers are usually located between the light source and the negative carrier in an enlarger to prevent the filter from distorting the image on the film.

Filter factor – A number used to calculate the effect a particular filter will have on exposure.

Filter pack – The total collection of filters in an enlarger. The filter pack is adjusted by increasing or decreasing the densities of the filters within it.

Fixer – A chemical that prevents the image on film or printing paper from fading by removing undeveloped silver compounds. Sometimes called *hypo.*

Focal length – The distance from the optical centre of a lens to the point behind the lens where a sharp image forms when the lens is focused on infinity. The focal length of the lens on an enlarger must project an image large enough to cover the paper on which the image is to be printed.

Focusing – The process of adjusting a lens so that it projects the sharpest image of which it is capable onto a sheet of printing paper.

Fog – Reduced contrast on film or printing paper caused either by stray light or by the action of chemicals. Film that is exposed to light before fixing has been completed becomes fogged.

***f*-stop** – (1) A numerical description of the size to which the aperture of a lens is set. The specific number represents the ratio between the diameter of the opening and the focal length of the lens. (2) A description of the difference in the intensity of light, as when one light intensity is said to differ from another by a certain number of *f*-stops.

Grade – See Contrast grade.

Grain – Clumps of metallic silver that always form on film or prints. With fine-grained film, the grain is barely discernible to the naked eye. With grainy film, the clumps are readily apparent. Film grain increases with film speed. (See Film speed.)

Hardening fixer – A fixer used to counteract the softness that photographic emulsions develop during processing.

Heat-absorbing glass – A sheet of glass inserted between the light source and the negative carrier in an enlarger to protect negatives and transparencies from the effects of the heat produced by the enlarger bulb.

High contrast – See Contrast.

High-contrast film – Film that converts all tones of grey to either pure black or pure white, depending on the shade of the original tone (e.g. Litho film.)

Highlight detail – Discernible features present in the lightest positions of a photograph. (See Shadow detail.)

Hypo – See Fixer.

Hypo eliminator – A chemical used after a hypo clearing agent to remove the last vestiges of processing chemicals from a print.

Intensifier – A chemical used to improve a negative which is not dense enough. (See Density.)

Internegative – A negative, prepared by copying a frame of reversal film, that is used to make a positive print.

ISO – A film speed rating which follows the convention introduced by the International Standards Organization. ISO numbers will eventually replace ASA and DIN ratings. (See ASA.)

Latent image – The potential but not yet developed image contained by silver halide crystals that have been exposed to light.

Lens opening – See Aperture.

Light-sensitive – A description for materials containing chemicals that change when exposed to light.

Magenta – One of the secondary colours that form the foundation of the subtractive method of colour production. Magenta filters block green light but allow red light and blue light to pass.

Masking frame – A device that holds printing papers flat when enlarging. Some frames have movable blades to permit cropping and also create white borders.

Multigrade – See Variable contrast paper.

Multiple exposure – A technique whereby two or more separate images are exposed on a single sheet of printing paper or film.

Negative carrier – A device which holds a negative or transparency flat and in the proper position within the enlarger while an exposure is being made.

Negative film – Film containing images which, when projected onto positive (not colour-reversal) printing paper, will produce positive images.

Neutral density – The result of combining equal densities of yellow, magenta, and cyan filters. The presence of neutral density decreases light intensity but does not affect colour.

Normal lens – A lens of focal length approximately equal to the diagonal of the film size. With 35mm film, normal lenses are about 50mm in focal length.

Orthochromatic – A description for films that do not respond to certain wavelengths of light. Orthochromatic films can be used in the presence of a safelight of the appropriate wavelength. (See Panchromatic.)

Over-exposure – A condition wherein more light has reached a frame of film or a sheet of printing paper than the amount required to form the best possible image.

Oxidation – The action of oxygen on a photographic chemical that results in the deterioration of the chemical's strength and ability to function properly.

Panalure – A printing paper sensitive to colour for making black and white prints from colour negatives.

Panchromatic A description for films that respond to all wavelengths of light in the visible spectrum. (See Orthochromatic.)

Paper weight – A measurement of a paper's relative thickness. Papers are designated as light (or single) weight, medium weight, and heavy (or double) weight.

Primary colours – The colours blue, green, and red. By mixing the primary colours in various combinations, any colour in the visible spectrum can be produced.

Print – A photographic image produced on a sheet of photographic printing paper.

Printing paper – A paper that has been coated with one or more light-sensitive emulsion layers and that will produce an image when properly exposed to light and processed.

Processing drum – See Drum processer.

Pull-processing – A procedure whereby film that has been shot at an ASA speed lower than that assigned by the manufacturer is developed for a shorter time than normal.

Push-processing – A procedure whereby film that has been shot at an ASA speed higher than that assigned by the manufacturer is developed for a longer time than normal.

Quartz-halogen lamp – A lamp, usually 12 or 24 volt, that produces a high-intensity light characterized by great consistency throughout the life of the lamp.

RC paper – See Resin-coated paper.

Reciprocity effect – A characteristic of film whereby a correct exposure occurs at a variety of easily predictable combinations of lens aperture and exposure time. At very long or very short exposure times, the relationship between lens aperture and shutter speed becomes erratic, a situation referred to as *reciprocity failure.*

Reciprocity failure – See Reciprocity effect.

Reducer – A chemical that improves a negative that is too dense to print well by removing some of the silver that forms the image. (See Density.)

Replenisher – A chemical added to a developer or other processing solution in order to return the solution to full chemical strength so that it can be reused.

Resin-coated (RC) paper – Photographic paper which has been chemically treated to restrict the amount of moisture it will absorb.

Resolving power – (1) A film's ability to produce fine detail in an image. (2) A lens's ability to project a sharp image.

Resolution – See Resolving power.

Reticulation – A wrinkled or cracked effect on film or prints created by exposing a photographic emulsion alternately to hot and cold temperature extremes.

Retouching – Improving or otherwise changing a negative or print by applying paint, ink, pencil, or bleach to portions of the emulsion or by etching the emulsion with a blade.

Reversal film – a film which produces a positive transparency by direct processing.

Safelight – A lamp that produces light of a wavelength to which a particular light-sensitive material does not respond. The safelight therefore provides visible illumination that does not affect the photographic image.

Sandwiching – Placing two or more transparencies or negatives together, then projecting light through the combination.

Secondary colours – See Complementary colours.

Shadow detail – Discernible features present in the darkest areas of a photograph. (See Highlight detail.)

Shelf life – The period of time during which properly cared-for chemicals can be stored without significant deterioration occurring.

Silver halides – Compounds of silver that convert to metallic silver and become black when exposed to light and chemically processed.

Slide – The name given to a transparency when it has been mounted for projection.

Spotting – Retouching small areas of a print to cover defects. (See Retouching.)

Squeegee – A rubber-edged device that removes excess water when passed over the surface of a print and thereby promotes rapid drying.

Squeegee tongs – Tongs with rubber strips attached that can be passed over both sides of a strip of film simultaneously to remove excess water and thereby promote fast drying.

Stabilizer – A chemical used in colour processing to improve the stability of the dyes in the emulsion and to act as a wetting agent. (See Wetting agent.)

Stock solution – A reserve quantity of a chemical solution.

Stop – Another and more popular word for aperture.

Stop bath – A chemical, usually acetic acid, that halts the action of the developer and prevents contamination of subsequent chemicals.

Subtractive colours – The colours yellow, magenta, and cyan. Also called *complementary or secondary colours.*

Subtractive method – A method of producing colours that relies on the ability of yellow, magenta, and cyan filters to block certain colours and pass others. By combining the filters in various patterns, any colour in the visible spectrum can be produced from white light. (See Complementary colours.)

Surge marks – Irregularities in development that occur around the sprocket holes in film, caused by developer flowing too rapidly through the holes due to excessive agitation.

Test print – A sample print made for the purpose of determining the correct exposure, paper contrast grade, or filtration to be used to make the final print.

Texture screen – A mesh that is placed in contact with a negative or transparency in order to produce a pattern across the surface of the print.

Toning – The process of affecting or replacing the silver image on a black and white print in order to add colour to the image and/or to prevent it from deteriorating.

Transparency – Usually a colour reversal, but sometimes a frame of black and white film giving a positive image. Transparencies are viewed by transmitted light, as from a projector. (See Slide.)

Tungsten light – The light produced by incandescent bulbs.

Ultra-violet (UV) filter – A filter used in colour printing that prevents colour shifts induced by ultra-violet light.

Under-exposed – A condition wherein less light has reached a frame of film or a sheet of printing paper than the amount required to form the best possible image.

Variable-contrast filters – Filters designed to be used with Multigrade paper.

Variable-contrast paper – Black and white printing paper, the grade of which is determined by the colour of the light used to project an image onto the paper. The colour of the light and hence the paper grade is controlled by variable-contrast filters. Commonly known as Multigrade.

Viewing filters – Devices through which a colour print can be viewed and which indicate the colour filtration adjustments needed to produce a print with correct colour balance. (See Colour balance.)

Water bath – A pool of water that has been adjusted to a specific temperature. Chemical containers and processing tanks placed in the water bath adapt to its temperature.

Wet mounting – Techniques of affixing prints to mounting surfaces by the use of liquid or aerosol adhesives.

Wet side – The portions of a darkroom devoted to processes that involve the use of liquids.

Wetting agent – A chemical that decreases the surface tension of water and thereby promotes rapid drying and prevents the formation of water spots. It is usually used on negatives.

White light – Light composed of all wavelengths in the visible spectrum.

Yellow – One of the complementary colours that form the foundation of the subtractive method of colour production. Yellow filters block blue light but allow red light and green light to pass.

INDEX